LIBERATING NORTH CHINA 1945

A CHINA MARINE'S STORY

WILLIAM HOOK

ISBN-13: 978-1500282950 (CreateSpace –Assigned)

ISBN-10: 1500282952

CONTENTS

PROLOGUE

In 1954 I had carved out a career with IBM in the United States and, in 1974, was appointed to a position, which required me to liaise between The IBM America/Far East Corporation (A/FE) headquarters in North Tarrytown, New York and its subsidiaries in eleven countries rimming the western Pacific.

On a Cathay Pacific flight from Sydney to Hong Kong I was seated next to a Polish gentleman named Peter Fischer, who had migrated to Australia and established an import/export business based in Sydney. During in-flight talks I revealed that I had served in the US Marine Corps in Tientsin (now Tianjin) in China and participated in the surrender of North China from the Japanese in 1945 on behalf of the Allied powers. He pricked up his ears and, eyes sparkling, told me that his Russian secretary had lived in Tientsin and had migrated to Australia when the communists took over North China in 1949. Being seated next to this man was one of those chance meetings that can only be described as fortuitous - it was destined to enrich the latter part of my life more than I could ever have envisioned.

On my next visit to Sydney Peter introduced me to his secretary who told me she knew of only one other person who had migrated to Australia from Tientsin - a German woman who had been married to a Latvian journalist. To my great surprise it turned out to be Marianne Reil who, with her husband Eric, were the first European civilians I met in Tientsin. I was 20 years old at that time and I estimated that they were in their late 20s or early 30s. They became my surrogate mother and father and we were very close. Eric had since moved to Japan and Marianne and her mother, an accomplished opera singer who was very popular in China, moved to Australia. I guessed the marriage had fallen apart but I knew no more than that. When I phoned Marianne I asked if she remembered a young Marine whom she had befriended in Tientsin. Her immediate response was: 'Is this my Billy?' We planned a reunion.

To my disappointment Marianne had become somewhat a recluse as her separation from Eric had taken its toll. She was not interested in rekindling our friendship - no doubt my visit had awakened memories of a happier time in her life. Marianne's mother had numerous friends, including Joan Stanbury, a journalist who had been Miss Australia, 1959. Marianne introduced me to Joan and we found that we enjoyed many of the same things, particularly theater. As the years slipped by, our friendship strengthened - as she would say, we have been 'mates' for many years. On my numerous trips to Australia, I would contact Joan and she always included me in whatever she was doing in her busy life. I was a welcome guest at her dinner parties, trips to the country and other activities and sometimes we enjoyed a restaurant meal together or would take in an opera or a musical at the famed Sydney Opera House.

When I retired from IBM in 1981, I established a consultancy in Singapore where I met and married Sally. My business took me through the same territory I had enjoyed in my IBM days so I often found myself traveling to Australia. On some trips, I would take Sally along. I usually holed up at a hotel where I would teach courses as part of my consultancy while Sally would stay at Joan's home - so they also became 'mates'.

Joan is an inveterate - and passionate - traveler and often came through Singapore so we had the pleasure of seeing her quite frequently. Over the years the friendship grew closer and today we count her as one of our nearest and dearest.

Because of Marianne - and my discussing my World War II history with her - Joan knew of my experiences as a member of the 17-man team of Marines who entered North China shortly after the signing of the surrender documents on the USS Missouri in Tokyo Bay. The assignment of this advance party of the US Marine Corps III Amphibious Corps was to establish relations with the Japanese Imperial Army, which occupied North China and to accept the surrender of North China from Japan on behalf of the Allied Forces. The surrender ceremony took place in Tientsin in October 1945.

This was a little known and unique slice of history and Joan was constantly urging me to write about my China experience.

For almost two decades I lived in the wonderful island country of Singapore, working in a number of different businesses and, after a few attempts at retirement, tried once again in the mid-1990s. Unfortunately restlessness set in. My wife Sally and I decided a change of scenery would be beneficial so we packed up and moved to the United States in 1999. My nephew, Joe Messina, had a wholesale food business and I had helped him in the overall management of his company from time to time. He decided to dispose of that business and bought a 108-acre farm in the rolling countryside outside the town of Valley Falls, north of Albany, NY. We joined him there and spent our days playing a lot of tennis and, in the winter, skiing at Bromley Mountain in southwest Vermont, about an hour's drive from where we were living.

The Bromley resort is known as a 'family' mountain where folks from Massachusetts, Rhode Island, Connecticut, New York, northern New Jersey and Pennsylvania return year after year - many having holiday homes in the area. I had learned to ski at the age of 43 and, though a late learner, loved the sport. What I lacked in style I made up for in enthusiasm - and was delighted when Sally joined me on the slopes. A keen and very competitive tennis player, Sally embraced the new sport and, in a short time, became a competent skier. Life was good, but, again, I was getting disenchanted with retirement so I approached the Personnel Manager at Bromley and won a seasonal job no one else in the company wanted - Cash Manager. Sally and I moved to the Green Mountain state.

The town of Manchester, Vermont has about 4000 residents, two stoplights, two roundabouts and several up-market factory outlet stores, which attract shoppers from far and wide. When we first moved it became apparent that the stores did not have alteration departments and getting clothes altered to fit was a problem for the outlet staff. Since sewing is a favorite hobby of Sally's she decided to open a limited business doing clothing alterations.

When I wrapped up my job at Bromley at the end of each skiing season, Sally suspended her little business and we took off for two to three months at our home in Singapore - often sneaking off to visit Joan and other good friends in Australia.

All of this activity allowed me to put the book in a basket labelled 'Procrastination' - although Joan kept bugging me to get on with it. English-speaking Sally is of Chinese heritage and is fluent in Mandarin and Cantonese, as well as Hakka, Hokkien and Malay. Although she was born in Malaysia and is a Singapore citizen she had never been to home of her forebears. Finally, in 2008, we decided to take a trip to China - and that was how the seeds for this book, already sewn, started to grow.

For Sally it was an adventure, for me it was a journey down memory lane. I sought to re-discover whatever architectural remnants were left from the first time I was in Tianjin (Tientsin in those days).

We had booked into a hotel in Beijing and took the train to Tianjin for a one-day visit. I was particularly interested in finding the house I occupied with six other Marines on Race Course Road; the office building which was Headquarters of the III Amphibious Corps and the hotel which first accommodated General Worton and the 16 other officers and enlisted men who accompanied him on the mission. My wife thought I was quite a dreamer to expect that these three locations would still be there after 66 years. Being the eternal optimist, I clung to hope.

The office building we occupied was a very substantial structure and I had the idea that it might still be useful just as it was. The Astor House Hotel had been built in 1863 and was the leading hotel in Tientsin. It had a rich history through the years and I had hoped that it might possibly have remained, perhaps as a landmark.

The house had its own story. The high-ranking officers of the III Amphibious Corps occupied homes in the plush area on Race Course Road. I was a driver for the Colonel who was the G-1 of the Corps. There were six other drivers who also drove for Colonels. One of our guys, Corporal Jerry Labounty was a close friend of mine and had served as a stenographer for the top brass. Jerry was a pushy guy and used his influence with the Commanding General to get the go ahead to rent a house near where the Colonels lived. The property he found was the former residence of the French Ambassador. It was a three-story structure with 23 rooms. Each of us had a bedroom, living room and a private bathroom. Once again, it had been a very substantial building and I felt that it might have survived the re-development of Tianjin. Tianjin, the third largest city in China, has been modernized but while the city is very up-to-date, it has also retained much of its rich history. We will re-visit these places later.

On this, our first trip, Sally and I made our way to the Central Train Station in Beijing and fought through an uncontrolled mob to purchase tickets. Sally's fluency in the language made travel in China a whole lot easier but did not eradicate the pushing and shoving. Once we had our tickets, we fought our way onto the train for the two-and-a-half hour journey to Tianjin. It was a cold, rainy day in April. We were unable to buy round-trip tickets so decided to buy our return trip tickets as soon as we got off the train in Tianjin although we would be leaving later in the day. The ticket office was outside the station so Sally, bless her, braved her way into the crowd of like-minded passengers enduring the pushing and shoving in the miserable rain.

Once we overcame that hurdle, we made our way by taxi to the Renaissance Hotel for a cup of hot coffee and a snack to thaw out. I chose that hotel since it was at the base of Race Course Road, where I wanted to start my search. My first quest was to find that lovely house, which I felt sure would still be there. We drove up one street and down another but came up with a complete zero. I wasted too much time in this endeavor - in the cold and rain - and was very disappointed.

I suggested that we find a nice restaurant, have a good meal, then make our way back to the train station to await our return train. With the help of a taxi driver, we were taken to a restaurant called 'Little Lamb' and had a superb meal of lamb, noodles and hot green tea. That made things a little better.

We got back to the station much too early for the reserved train so we ventured into a near-by coffee shop. Sally chatted with the lady proprietor and told her of our quest

11

and disappointment. We vowed to come back another time and resume our search, hopefully better prepared. The charming lady told Sally that there was a place where old folks stayed and gave us the phone number. She reasoned that some of those folks might remember the old days and support our task. Plans for the rest of our China visit were set in stone, but we knew we would have to revisit Tianjin in the not-too-distant future.

The train ride back was not too bad but at the Beijing end, again we ran into a challenging scene. It was necessary to go outside the station to get a taxi - in the cold and rain. There must have been 10 times as many people as there were taxis and no queues.

As we mingled in the mob, we suddenly realized that a young man was holding an umbrella over our head. He told us that he would help us to get a taxi. As an experienced resident, he knew how to 'work the scene' and soon we had a cab. When Sally gave the taxi driver the address of our hotel, our benefactor said his apartment was not far from where we were going so we all piled into the cab and were on our way. That was the beginning of a new relationship with Chuck Yu, a gentleman who we are honored to call a friend. Actually, Chuck's heart-warming assistance was not unusual - we were the recipients of other acts of generosity in this beautiful city. Many citizens of Beijing go out of their way to offer a friendly hand to visitors. A number of times on the underground railway younger folks offered us their seats.

We vowed that we would return to China again to resume my quest for unanswered questions, which lingered in my mind.

CHAPTER ONE

THE CHILDHOOD YEARS

Nothing in my upbringing indicated that I would, within a few years of graduating from Grammar School in 1940, become a proud member of the US Marine Corps - which is, in my view, the finest military organization in the world. My intention was to pursue a career in commerce. Fate has a way of intervening.

I was born upstate New York in the village of Norton Hill, which was - and still is - not much more than a whistle-stop in Greene County. As was the custom, midwives attended births so I was born at home on June 16, 1925. My father was a butcher who sold meat from a horse-drawn wagon, which travelled from house to house throughout the countryside. He was a hopeless alcoholic who appeared not to care for his children and who treated my mother badly. His father, also a butcher, was a wealthy man who retired at the age of 50 and allowed my father the luxury of bearing little responsibility for his actions. My grandfather bought a house for our family, but did not trust my father enough to deed the property to him.

I have only a couple of recollections from those years. One was when I was lying in a hammock and a pig wandered underneath, almost flipping me on to the ground. The other could have had more serious consequences. I guess I was left in the care of my older siblings on the second story of our house and somehow fell out of the window, barely missing a chopping block with an axe embedded in it. I landed on the grass, but still carry a scar on my leg from the incident. Death by defenestration could have nipped this whole story in the bud.

My mother took as much abuse as she could tolerate from my father and, seeking a better life for us all, bundled up her four children - Bob (10), Jean (6) Betty (4) and me, aged three - and took us to stay with her sister in Jersey City, New Jersey. Though my parents had separated, throughout the years we maintained a warm relationship with my paternal grandparents and therefore saw my father from time to time. The relationship was neither a hostile, nor a loving one.

When sober my father was an artist with a butchers' knife. He could take a side of beef and produce the most marvelous cuts of meat. This skill earned him good jobs and even provided the entrée to a job in the Army Air Corps during World War II. Unfortunately his bouts of sobriety never lasted long and were his undoing. His father and his brothers were all butchers and the name 'Hook' was

15

synonymous with 'fine butchery'. They all did well and retired to live comfortably for the rest of their lives. My brother Bob also took up the trade. Bob had been plagued with a troublesome stomach, which he picked up during the war and was not in good health. His penchant for the same sauce which afflicted my father, led to his early death leaving a fine wife and three children.

Many times throughout the years I tried to help my dad. He was living upstate New York, not too far from the old homestead, which his older brother, my Uncle Joe, had bought from my grandfather. If my dad had stayed off the booze, I am sure Uncle Joe would have cared for him, but, because of his drinking, he considered that 'the devil had hold of him' and chose not to associate much with him.

A few years later, when I hadn't seen my father for some time - I was working in New York City - the vice president of the bank my father dealt with phoned me at my office. He chastised me for allowing my father to be imprisoned for six months on a charge of vagrancy. Baffled, I sought an explanation.

It appeared that, while inebriated, my father had walked into traffic on a busy highway and was brushed by a car. He had superficial wounds, but nothing serious. The police offered to take him home, but he convinced them that he could make it on his own so they departed. Instead of going home he went back into the bar for a little more 'juice' before again attempting to walk home. A second car brushed him and the same policemen came to the scene. They had had enough and took him into custody. The next day the whole sorry story was spilled out in court and the judge sentenced him to six months in jail. Uncle Joe thought it was a good idea as it might teach him a lesson.

Fortunately the banker did not share that view so he phoned me. I drove for three hours to the town where dad had been sentenced and pleaded with the judge to release him rather than send him to prison. Despite all his failing as a husband and father, he was not a felon and I did not wish to see him incarcerated with criminals. The judge agreed to release him - in my custody - so I took him home with me and sobered him up (not an easy task). Incidentally, the judge, Frank Tate became and is to this day a very dear friend. I found a rehabilitation establishment on a farm which was organized and managed by some dedicated people who had beaten alcoholism and who were keen to help others in the same predicament. The fee was reasonable but required that everyone living there did their share of daily jobs. Dad was rather work-shy so, within a short time, was seeking my help - to get him out of there.

At this stage I was running out of options, but did manage to find him a mobile home located in a respectable trailer park with warm and friendly neighbors. He settled there quite happily.

In the meantime my life had changed and I was involved in a lot of international travel. I did not see much of him - in fact, I was in the Far East on assignment when he passed away and found it impossible to attend his funeral.

My mother had worked in the film industry before she was married so, following the separation from my father, it was not hard for her to get a job. Although earning a decent wage, raising four children while working was challenging for her. She was a tireless employee - often continuing on beyond normal working hours - but did her best to make a home for us. She was an excellent cook and after slaving at the 'coalface' would come home and prepare dinner for us. Although she demonstrated her profound love in many ways, she was also a firm disciplinarian. For instance, when we sat down to eat she put the food on each of our plates and we had to eat everything before we were offered second helpings. We also had our chores to perform - including making our own beds and keeping our bedrooms clean and tidy - and if we got lax a smack on the butt was not uncommon. In the early years Bob and I shared a room and Jean and Betty shared another. Although not of the faith, Mom honored her commitment to my Catholic father and enrolled us in a Catholic school, which gave us a good foundation for a Christian life.

After a couple of years of living with relatives we moved into a rented house and in the following years moved a couple of times, still within Jersey City and always in nice homes and good neighborhoods. What my mother couldn't give us by being with us during the day she made up for with kindness and thoughtfulness. Her weekends were devoted to housecleaning, laundry and ironing.

As we grew older Mom put Jean, Betty and me into a fine boarding school in the Bronx - across the road from the Yankee Stadium. Bob was sent to a working farm school in upstate New York then to a horse farm/school in New Hampshire. For many years during summer school holidays, my sister Betty and I took a Greyhound bus upstate to where my maternal grandmother had a boarding house. We worked waiting on the dinner tables, washing dishes, cleaning rooms, keeping the grounds clean and anything else that Grandma required. She made her own beer and stored it in the basement where it was cool. Often, warning me against stealing, she would send me down to get a bottle for her. Although we worked hard, we always managed to get a couple of hours off after lunch to go over to a nearby creek to swim. When we got a bit older we also rented bicycles in the evening and often rode to another village about five miles away. One year my grandmother 'farmed me out' to another boarding house where I worked as a dishwasher. My pay was a dollar a day, which she

19

promptly confiscated. She was not aware that some of the boarders gave me small tips so I had a little spending money.

When I was nine years old one of my mother's sisters, who had a farm outside Amsterdam, New York, offered to care for me so, for two-and-a-half years, I lived with her. During the summer I was up at the crack of dawn with her husband, my Uncle Al. While he was busy in the barn I went out to bring the 31 cows in for milking. He milked 16 and I milked the rest. This was done by hand, but I admit I got the easy milkers while he did the tougher ones. During winter the cows stayed in the barn overnight but I still milked my 15 cows before walking two miles to school. On weekends in the winter months we would go out to ponds and cut ice for storage in our icehouse. The ice was packed in sawdust to keep it from melting as it had to last through the summer months. We had no electricity and I slept in a loft over the kitchen. We had a battery-operated radio to which we listened on long winter nights while we sat round the dining room table, picking particles out of the wool we had sheared off the sheep the previous summer.

My life on the farm ended when my aunt ran off with the hired man and my distraught uncle sent me back to New Jersey to my mom. She sent me to Public School #11 which was across the road from a grocery store. I got a job delivering groceries after school and all day on Saturday for

75 cents a week, plus tips. My biggest tipper was the boss's wife who gave me 25 cents. Most tips were five or 10 cents.

Mom sent me to live with friends in Brooklyn - which was pretty nice - until I graduated from elementary school then she and I moved to a small apartment on 65th Street, New York City, off Central Park West.

The following summer I took a job as a parking lot attendant in Jersey City, NJ, which was some distance from our home. At the end of the summer I enrolled in the High School of Commerce in New York City but fate put some hurdles in my way which made my continuing education difficult, in fact, nigh on impossible.

My mother was employed by Deluxe Studios, a subsidiary of 20th Century Fox. It was a good job but she became involved in a union dispute and lost her job for more than a year. Consequently my $16.00 a week pay packet as a parking lot attendant, plus tips, was an important ingredient in the financial viability of our family - we paid $7.00 a week rent. As my job was from 4pm until midnight, I rode the tube train from Jersey City to 34th street in New York City, and then walked to 65th Street in order to save the five-cent subway fare. I have fond memories of dining, quite regularly, on lamb stew which was about the cheapest meat we could afford. Unlike many Americans, I still enjoy the flavor of lamb.

I attempted doing my night job and attending school in the daytime but often played 'hooky' because I was too tired to make it to school. The Board of Education did not like that very much but, on learning of our difficulties, sought a solution. They made a deal with my mother for me to take an address in Jersey City, thereby relieving me of the obligation of attending school in New York City. Problem solved! Good fortune came our way about a year later. Mom got her job back and I got a full-time job with the Standard Oil Company of New Jersey (Esso) as a seaman on an oil tanker, which plied the east coast of North and South America.

CHAPTER TWO

THE EARLY WORKING YEARS

The Standard Oil Company of New Jersey had a fleet of tankers that was registered in Panama - a 'flag of convenience' - and therefore not party to wage regulations and the other employment requirements, including insurance and holiday pay, of the United States. Perhaps my age, 16, had something to do with it, but I neither knew nor cared at the time.

For a lad of my age life at sea was busy, jam packed with excitement and full of interest - and I was eager to learn. Little was I to know that events in the Pacific were rapidly unfolding that would alter the whole course of world history and, along with millions of other Americans, propel me along a path that I would never have dreamed possible.

On my first trip with the Standard Oil Company we sailed from Bayonne, New Jersey - our 'home' port - to Caripito, Venezuela. We carried a load of refined oil, which was discharged, and then we loaded up with crude to take to Rio de Janeiro for refinement. Off the coast of Pernambuco, Brazil, I was enjoying a Sunday morning visit to 'Sparks', the radio operator. As we chatted - I questioned him

23

relentlessly about his work, life at sea and every other thing I could think of, relishing his years of experience - his ear was constantly tuned into the dots and dashes of Morse code coming in on his radio. Suddenly he held up his hand to silence me and shouted: 'Shut up. I have a very important message coming in'. He told me the news as he jotted down some notes then jumped up and said he had to go to the bridge and see the Captain. I ambled aft to the mess hall where off-duty sailors sat around drinking coffee and telling tall stories. They greeted me with: 'Any news?' Completely unaware of the significance of my story I told them that Sparks had just gone to tell the Captain that the Japanese had bombed some place called Pearl Harbor. My reward was a lesson in geography and the chilling revelation that we were, effectively, at war.

Following orders from Bayonne we proceeded to Rio de Janeiro, discharged our cargo of crude and waited a few days while company executives worked out how to cope with running a shipping company, carrying highly volatile cargoes, while at war. They ordered us to paint the porthole covers black and run without lights to our next port of call. We loaded up with refined oil and also spent time scrubbing out a few of the ship's storage holds. We completed that job by coating them with a clay-like substance so we could fill them with water to take to our next destination, Aruba, an island of the Lesser Antilles, 17 miles north of the coast of

Venezuela. Fresh water was in short supply on the island so what we brought in was essential for their well being.

At that time German submarines were very active in the North and South Atlantic Oceans but, until then, were not attacking ships flying US or Panamanian flags. On December 11, 1941, when the United States declared war on Germany, all that changed. We were now the prime targets for a fleet of very clever U-boat captains.

We made it to Aruba, discharged our cargo, reloaded with crude oil and headed for Bayonne.

In the months that followed the waters in which I sailed became progressively more and more treacherous. The German submarines were very busy and America lost a lot of ships. We tried all sorts of tactics, but the U-boat commanders always seemed to be one step ahead of us. Our ships were sunk in such shallow waters that soon the seascapes off the US east coast were dotted with the masts of ships sticking out of the water. It seemed that no sooner were you out of sight of one that another would be in view.

For us there was a little respite. Ships sailing under Panamanian registration were not subject to the same scrutiny as US ships. Imbued with the work ethic by my mother, I constantly begged other sailors and mates to teach me the skills of seamanship - and they were eager to share their knowledge. Despite tales of rough and tough guys, the men I sailed with were mostly serious-minded men who had chosen the hard but reasonably well-paid life at sea to provide for their families. On my first trip I was a Mess Boy; on the second I shipped out as an Ordinary Seaman and before long qualified for the position of Able Bodied Seaman - a career trajectory which was probably unprecedented in those days, but, to my joy, a reality. A major factor in my rise in status was my natural - and uncanny - ability to steer unwieldy tankers, most of which were built in the 1915 - 1930 era. From whence this odd talent came I had no idea. The ship I sailed on most was the MS J. A. Mowinckel, built in Italy in 1930.

Only Able Bodied Seamen were permitted to man the wheel on these giant ships and steering them could be very tricky. Thirty seconds elapsed from the time you turned the wheel in the wheelhouse until the rudder actually began to move. The helmsman then had to spin the wheel back to amidships and beyond to keep the ship on the right track. Currents and other ship traffic complicated the exercise. Steering within the confines of New York Harbor was especially challenging. There was only one pilot in the New York City area qualified to bring the Mowinckel in and out of that port. After a few trips, whenever he came on board, if I was not already on the wheel, he would say: 'Vere's de kid? Get him up here'. We had formed a working relationship and he had confidence in my abilities.

One event, even in retrospect, makes me tremble. In our desperate attempts to avoid the German U-boats we pulled off all sorts of stunts. We travelled through the Intracoastal Waterway when it was feasible and once, when sailing from Bayonne to Nova Scotia, plotted a circuitous course and, instead of going out to the Atlantic Ocean through the lower bay, we went through the upper bay - across New York Harbor. This meant avoiding incoming and outgoing vessels as well as the large Staten Island Ferries, passing the Statue of Liberty and Governors Island and entering the East River to access the Atlantic via Long Island Sound.

Getting across the Harbor was nail biting, but a more testing moment was in the wings. Just past Governors Island is the entrance to the East River - and the U.S. Navy Yard in Brooklyn is not too far from the mouth of the river. With extreme caution we sailed under the Brooklyn Bridge, then under the Manhattan Bridge when, without warning, the battleship USS North Carolina powered past on our port side, cut across our bow and headed into the Navy Yard. Those guys did not seem to be the least bit interested in a bulky tanker with comparatively next-to-no manoeuvrability. I had to steer hard to port to avoid ramming into her stern, then around to starboard to get back on course. My heart was in my mouth but I couldn't get too upset over the perceived indiscretion of the crew of the battleship because, as they passed right under my nose, all hands were on deck for inspection. Pure patriotism washed over me as I saw all of those officers and sailors dressed in their finest white uniforms. I almost burst with pride at the sight of those splendid fighting men. Little did I know that I would be thrust into similar ranks in the not-too-distant future.

Our journey continued up the East River, under the 59th Street Bridge and barely sneaking by the island in the middle of the river as we prepared for the next challenge - Hell Gate. It was spring tides and the currents are notoriously tricky as there is a confluence of three different bodies of water. Holding the ship steady and maintaining way against the wind and the tide took all the skill I could muster. When we got into Long Island Sound we were rewarded with great views of Long Island on our starboard side and Connecticut and Rhode Island to the north. We sailed past Fishers Island and Block Island before poking our nose out into the mighty Atlantic, slipping to the south of Martha's Vineyard and Nantucket and hugging the coast of Cape Cod on our track north. Some 60-plus years later I would experience much joy and pleasure visiting these places.

To provide a modicum of protection we were armed with a three-inch gun, which was manned by US Navy sailors. On one occasion a German submarine surfaced in the middle of our convoy and a sailor - with an impossibly complicated

28

Greek name - dispatched it with a direct hit on the conning tower. The same gentleman told me that, while at Boot Camp roll call, the drill instructor would make a few attempts at saying his name and then resort to: 'The S.O.B. (my abbreviation) with the long name'.

A couple of personal issues were bothering me. One was that, with the US at war, I realized how vulnerable we tanker sailors were. The Navy simply did not have sufficient ships available to protect merchant fleets so sailing under any conditions was fraught with great danger. Sometimes we travelled in convoys - which provided the German U-boats with a smorgasbord to pick off ships at their leisure - while at other times we had one or two Canadian Corvettes as escorts. They were so slow that the merchant ships had to reduce speed in order for them to keep pace. I left the Mowinckel in July 1942 and it was torpedoed on the trip following my departure. It managed to limp into port and was repaired but later struck a mine and sank. Esso was eager to keep as many seamen as possible on the job so they kept offering incentives such as hazardous duty bonuses, many retroactive. In short, I was rolling in money. I had allotted my entire paycheck to my mother and still had plenty of income through the bonuses.

The other issue that worried me was that while I was earning big money my brother, Bob, had enlisted with the US Marine Corps and was paid a measly $21 a month. The

29

disparity tugged at my conscience, I felt guilty receiving such riches when he was laying his life on the line for a mere pittance. I decided to do something about it. With my mom's permission, I reported to the Church Street recruiting office in New York City and joined the Marines. Bob had shipped out with the 8th Marine Regiment of the 1st Marine Division and saw fierce combat on Guadalcanal, our first major offensive against the Japanese. I never regretted my decision although I felt pangs of self-reproach for leaving my former shipmates, none of whom survived World War II. I lost every one of them.

CHAPTER THREE

BECOMING A MARINE

Boot Camp on Parris Island is legendary in the Marine Corps but I thoroughly enjoyed the rigorous training and worked hard at it. However, in my enthusiasm to join the fighting forces I had overlooked giving Esso a notice of resignation. A letter arrived from them advising that I had been selected for Third Officer training and I was to report to New London, Connecticut for duty.

A Third Officer at the tender age of 17? I could not believe it - nor did I know what to do. The matter was quickly resolved. I took the letter to the Commanding Officer of our unit. His response was classical. He said: 'Son, I am going to introduce a term, which you may not have heard before but will become part of your vocabulary throughout your time in the Marine Corps. The term is 'this is what you call tough shit and your ass belongs to the Marines'. Memorable indeed.

Many times I have been asked to describe the Marine Corps Boot Camp - its reputation is awesome. After the months I had spent as sea, often in physically and mentally demanding circumstances and certainly, during the war, in gut-wrenching fear of being torpedoed, hitting a mine or taking an explosive missile amidships, I found Boot Camp an entirely different sort of challenge. Our drill instructors were the most rugged guys you would ever want to encounter, but, contrary to much ballyhoo voiced and written about them, they were not cruel. What they put us through was more like tough love. Hard encouragement may be another way of describing it.

Perhaps a little story would illustrate why I have such a positive opinion of my Boot Camp experience. I had a very difficult time mastering the bayonet course where we were required to deal with a series of dummies, pushing away their bayonet-mounted rifles and delivering a fatal blow. A deep-seated revulsion of the act meant that I resisted coordinating the movements. Fearful that I might fail, I sneaked out of the barracks the night before the final examination - under a full moon - and ran the course over and over again, almost until dawn. After breakfast I ran the course for real and qualified without a hitch. Our drill instructor came over to me and put his arm around my shoulder. 'I watched you last night through my window and I knew that you were going to earn the honor of the title, United States Marine. I am proud of you.' He made me feel that I had entered Boot Camp as a boy and departed a man.

My first assignment was to the Communications School at Quantico, Virginia. In those days communications meant dots and dashes or field telephones. We heard that a student in Radio School had taken his own life the previous week owing to the cramming method of learning the skill of Morse code. Evidently it was a really stiff course. They asked for volunteers and I did not dive in. The second offer was Telephone School, which did not appear attractive either. There was no third choice. Those who hadn't volunteered were put on Mess Duty. For a while I was fearful I might be on permanent Mess Duty. The Communications School moved from Quantico to Hadnot Point, Camp Lejeune, North Carolina. We were the first unit to populate that new section.

The barracks housing our battalion was a string of buildings in a row. Shortly after we moved in, the first unit of a new breed of Marines moved into another row of buildings which was separated from us by a lightly-wooded area. We quickly learned that our neighbors were the first group of a very different breed of Marines - newly recruited women. Someone hung a not so nice title on them, the abbreviation of which was BAMs - Broad Ass Marines. I imagine there may have been a little hanky-panky going on but my personal experience with this new class of Marines was casual conversation, talking about hometowns, family life, etc. In other words I found them to be ladies.

CHAPTER FOUR

BEACH JUMPER UNIT #1

Somehow I managed to get off Mess Duty and was assigned
to a battalion awaiting permanent assignment into a regular
operating unit. Before long it came my way. The well-
known actor, Douglas Fairbanks Jr. had enlisted in the
Navy, smartly achieved the rank of Lieutenant Commander
and was working on a top-secret activity which the British
had developed. He travelled to England to learn more about
it – he confided that what they had demonstrated to him
'frightened the be-Jesus out of him'. However, he came
back with a proposal to form a special unit of Marines. As I
was awaiting assignment, I learned that the unit
Commander Fairbanks had established was accepting
volunteers. Its mission would not be revealed until all
volunteers became part of what was named Beach Jumper
Unit #1.

The purpose of this new unit was to create diversionary
tactics to lure the enemy away from intended landing sites.
With his theatrical background this was a tailor-made job
for Commander Fairbanks who had persuaded several film

sound technicians to give up their cushy jobs in Hollywood and enlist in the Marines. The Unit consisted of only 69 enlisted men and 16 officers. In addition to the sound technicians they required some regular Marines for assorted duties. I became a demolition specialist whose principal duty was to blow up our equipment when we had completed our mission or in the event that the enemy discovered our ruse.

After training on the East Coast we went to Treasure Island near San Francisco to await transport to the Pacific theater of war. Beach Jumper Unit #1 was put on a small freighter leased from the Dutch, with a handful of Navy guys, working mostly in food service and running a well-supplied Post Exchange (PX). Dutch civilian merchant seamen ran the ship. Secrecy was essential so we had no duties related to our mission on board and did not discuss what we were about to do with any of the crew or Navy personnel.

The trip was memorable for a number of reasons. The first was that we had all been paid just before leaving Treasure Island, but had no chance to spend our money in San Francisco before we shipped out. We had cash. Poker and blackjack became the primary activities.

The second unforgettable event was the failure of the refrigeration system - the freighter was ancient. The spoilt supply of meat, fish and vegetables became food for the sharks while we resorted to whatever canned goods were available. We ate a lot of beans and eggs.

As the gambling progressed two guys ended up with all the money on board. Because of the small number of people on the ship there was a great sense of fellowship and every day the guys with the money went to the PX store and bought up canned beans, sardines, boxes of crackers and whatever else was available and shared it with everyone. At the end of the voyage all the money was in the PX and tummies were satisfied.

The third reason I remember the trip so well was that there was only one movie on board which I think I watched every night. It was 'Casablanca'. By the end of the voyage I knew Humphrey Bogart's lines as well as he did.

We had sailed from Treasure Island to Noumea, New Caledonia and awaited the outcome of combat actions in the Solomon Islands. After a few weeks we got the thumbs-up signal and boarded a US Navy vessel to sail to Guadalcanal in the Solomon Islands, which was to be our home until we went into combat. We were holed up in a remote location away from the rest of the troops on the island - they were unaware of what we were doing and I don't think they cared, either.

The tools of Beach Jumper Unit #1 consisted mainly of recorded sounds of anchors dropping from ships, landing crafts, gunfire and various other audio effects that mimicked war-like activity. The Hollywood guys knew their stuff and had perfected recordings on steel wire, which spelled 'quality'. They even rigged up a loud speaker in a coconut tree so we could tune into 'Tokyo Rose', the woman who broadcast propaganda to American troops from Japan. Our main bases of operations were two specially equipped PT boats.

All our work was showcased to a collection of admirals, generals and other high-ranking officers one night on a remote beach. They were all seated and perhaps a little apprehensive about our ability to perform. A Navy ship had laid down a smoke screen parallel to the beach and we orchestrated our show behind the all-concealing wall of smoke. We began with the sound of shell fire (in an actual mission the shell fire would be real as warships would be firing over our heads to give the impression of an imminent landing) followed by sounds of ships dropping anchors, sounds of landing craft and a variety of other noises which would accompany a large force about to make a beachhead. After a time the smoke screen dissipated and all the big brass could see were our two PT boats bobbing on the surface beyond the breakers. The officers were impressed and we were to make our first thrust against the enemy on the island of Bougainville, the next target of the Fleet Marine Force, Pacific.

While on Guadalcanal the sound technicians were busy refining their performance while we 'ordinary' Marines honed our training. There was a fair amount of leisure time as well and some of us found things to do.

A buddy of mine who was from the southern part of the United States - where brewing moonshine was not uncommon - suggested the possibility of emulating the process on this far-flung Pacific island. Gullible and foolhardy, I signed on to the deal. With fewer than 100 men in the whole unit, we had a small mess tent where our meals were prepared and eaten. Adjacent to this tent was another open-sided tent where provisions were stored. As there was a constant threat of pilfering, a Marine guarded both the mess and the storage tent every night. His duty was to walk around the sites, keeping a sharp eye out for any illegal activity. Having pulled that duty we knew how long it took the sentry to make his rounds and, noting the amount of time he was on the opposite side of the units, we devised a plan.

One night we hid out of sight of the guard and waited for him to go around to the opposite side of the tents. One of us slipped into the storage tent and identified what we would steal. We were after any kind of dried fruit and sugar – elements that would work in the fermentation process. Silently we slipped out with our treasure and hid it amongst the coconut palms. It took several trips but, eventually, we had our ingredients.

The next day we carried the loot into the jungle where the manufacturing of our beverage was to take place. I had located an empty wooden nail keg, scrubbed it out and, under the direction of our learned Southern friend, set up our makeshift fermentation tank. As the beverage matured it required several transfers in the refinement process. As careful as we were I guess we were not bright enough to escape the eyes of other guys in the unit. Almost at the time the stuff was sufficiently refined to drink, it disappeared. A night or two later there was a big party in one of the tents. Although we protested we had to admit that we had been 'had'. And, it all being illegal, there was no way to seek justice. We chalked it up as a lesson well learned.

As we approached the time for our participation in the Bougainville campaign we were allotted specific roles. Part of the plan was to land three men from a rubber boat on the opposite side of the island 24 hours before 'Z' (Zero) hour - two sound technicians and one demolition specialist. At the appropriate time we were to play recordings emulating a variety of small arms fire, with the intent of diverting the Japanese away from the area where the 'real' landing was to be staged.

After a specified time - during which we expected the enemy to begin engaging the supposed forces we had mimicked - the equipment was to be destroyed by the demolition technician and the three men were to get back in the rubber boat and paddle out far enough for a submarine to pick them up. I could have been that demolition guy but, as John Steinbeck famously said: 'The best laid schemes of mice and men often go awry'.

At this point we 'grunts' - ordinary Marines - did not have access to every aspect of the planning and execution stages of the exercise. We will never know what went wrong, but this was the story that was leaked: In the final briefing before striking out on the campaign, Admiral Halsey commented that he had not seen a requisition for the rescue submarine. Somehow it had not been submitted. Halsey, one of my all-time heroes of this war then proclaimed that it was not right to leave three men stranded without an escape plan. He ordered the Beach Jumper Unit #1 be scratched from the operation. To me this was an example of leadership which tolerates no mistakes and is swift to remove the possibility of failure. Shortly afterwards the unit was disbanded.

While we had been playing 'make-believe' with the Beach Jumper Unit #1, there were other things going on in the Pacific theater of operations of which I was privileged to have first-hand knowledge. However, before delving into that I wish to explain why I believe it is difficult to get any records regarding the ill-conceived - or just ill fated - Beach

Jumper Unit #1.

While we were operational, our organization was classified 'Top Secret'. I do not believe that this classification had anything to do with the absence of historical data. My opinion is that the Marine Corps and the Navy wanted the sad saga of Beach Jumper Unit #1 simply to go away. Although the Navy did operate Beach Jumper Units, primarily in Europe, as far as the Marine Corps was concerned, it was just a bad dream. Although as a group we were out of business, I understand that some of the techniques we practiced were applied by the 2nd Marine Division to divert the enemy during the Okinawa campaign.

So what happened to the talented and highly trained members of the unit? I have no idea where the Hollywood group went but I ended up with some of the other Marines in a Casual Company performing an assortment of duties including the unloading of supply ships. We were all awaiting re-assignment to combat units.

When there are men unloading ships anywhere in the world it appears there is a built-in culture of pilfering - and it was no different with us despite the fact we belonged to an elite group, would have laid down our lives for our fellow servicemen and were in a theater of war. There was no market for Jeeps or trucks so they came ashore and were driven to their designated locations with no problems or losses. Beer, on the other hand, was a different story. Enlisted men could purchase small quantities of this beverage from the PX but additional supplies were in keen demand.

Surveillance was sharp during the unloading of ships, so creative measures had to be applied. In those pre-container days nets were lowered into the holds of the ship, loaded with cargo and brought up, over the side and on to the wharf where it was re-loaded on to trucks for transport to its destination. There was little opportunity to re-direct alcoholic beverages into the arms of thirsty Marines - or, at least, until someone came up with a novel idea. A case of beer would be brought up from the hold, carried to the sea-side of the ship and dropped into the water. Underneath the pier an alert individual on break would hear the splash, dive into the water and swim around the stern of the ship to retrieve the wayward cargo and guide it back under the pier where no one was watching. Those in the know would slip away from their jobs and partake of a few beers before returning to work. Sometimes some of the chaps went back to camp with a distinctly wobbly gait.

CHAPTER FIVE

BIRTH OF THE III AMPHIBIOUS CORPS

The Casual Company provided a supply of men to meet requests for other duties. A friend of mine had been tapped to work with an organization, which was gearing up for much bigger things - the headquarters of the newly formed III Amphibious Corps. His job was to run messages and materials from one office to another. He hated the job but I noticed that he always went to work in clean khakis and returned the same way so the job had some attraction, when compared with the dirty work of unloading ships. When he told me he was seeking a return to the Casual Company, I prevailed upon him to ask his commanding officer, a colonel, if I could replace him. Colonel Gale T Cummings was the G-I Officer of the Corps and could not care less about who the runner was. He agreed to my friend's request and I got the job. As the organization grew in scope and mission the job became permanent and I was grateful for the position.

This seemingly small incident in the whole jigsaw of my war service re-directed my Marine career path and I will be eternally grateful to that friend who, unknowingly, was responsible for such a pivotal point in my life. Colonel Cummings was one of the top six Colonels under the command of - and reporting to - Major General Roy S Geiger. Actually very few people were assigned to the Corps Headquarters. My guess is that the direct reports to the Commanding General and a handful of others were in that category. The rest reported to the Headquarters and Service Battalion of the III Amphibious Corps for housekeeping and services. The Corps then consisted of Divisions and other units, which came under its command for specific operations.

I am not an historian, nor do I profess to know about every aspect of military organization development. I do, however, have first-hand experience of some aspects of the formation of the III Amphibious Corps and, for posterity; wish to record the extent of my knowledge.

In this context a Corps was essentially a headquarters organization consisting of a Commanding General and the five major support offices: G-1 (Personnel); G-2 (Intelligence); G-3 (Operations); G-4 (Logistics) and G-5 (Civil Affairs). Divisions, regiments, battalions, air wings, artillery battalions and any other military organization, which could lend itself to a specific mission, came under the command of the 'Corps'.

The individual units under the command of a Corps tended not to identify themselves as part of the Corps as they viewed themselves as the operational unit and could not care less about organizational structure - nor were they inclined to have allegiance to a higher authority.

The creation of the III Amphibious Corps started with the First Marine Amphibious Corps (I MAC), which was created on October 1, 1942 in California. It was deployed to Hawaii and then to New Caledonia. Originally it was under the command of General Clayton B Vogel who served in that capacity until July 1943.

He was relieved by General Alexander Vandergrift, (who had been promoted to Lieutenant General). He had commanded the famed 1st Marine Division, which defeated the Japanese on Guadalcanal. He was instrumental in the planning of the next major conquest by the Marines in the Solomon Islands, the island of Bougainville.

Shortly after establishing a beachhead on Bougainville on November 1, 1943, General Vandergrift was recalled to Washington as Commandant of the Marine Corps designate.

Major General Roy S Geiger took over as Commanding General of the First Marine Amphibious Corps. General Geiger was the first Marine flyer to have served in World War I when, in 1919, he was awarded his first Navy Cross. Until taking command of the First Marine Amphibious

Corps most of his career was in aviation. During the battle for Guadalcanal he led the Cactus Air Force, which consisted of the combined Army, Navy and Marines as well as the 1st Marine Aircraft Wing.

Under his co-ordinate command 268 Japanese planes in aerial combat were shot down and many more damaged. The Cactus Air Force also sank six enemy vessels including three destroyers and one heavy cruiser and damaged another 18 ships including one heavy cruiser and five light cruisers.

General Geiger was awarded a Gold Star in lieu of a second Navy Cross for his service on Guadalcanal.

As Commander of the First Marine Amphibious Corps he continued the campaign on Bougainville until turning over the operation to the US Army Forces. For service in this campaign he was awarded the Distinguished Service Medal.

The First Marine Amphibious Corps was re-designated as the III Amphibious Corps on Guadalcanal in April 1944.

There is an interesting aspect in the build-up of the full-fledged Corps, which was preparing for its first combat operation since its formation. This fact struck me at the time and even more so as I recall that period of history.

The 4th Marine Regiment was first activated on April 14, 1914 in Puget Sound, Washington and Mare Island,

California Naval Yards under the command of Colonel Joseph Henry Pendleton. This action was a direct result of deteriorating relations at that time between the United States and Mexico. The Regiment fulfilled its role in the ensuing unrest and went on to serve the United States on land and on the sea for many years afterwards.

The 4th Marines was a well known and highly respected military regiment that served in China for many years. As World War II approached they were based in Shanghai - where they had been for the previous 15 years. In November 1941 President Roosevelt ordered the withdrawal of all Marine detachments in China. With a great deal of anguish over leaving their beloved Shanghai, these gallant Marines gathered up their gear and boarded the SS Harrison and the SS Madison for a journey into the unknown - at least for them.

Their destination was the Philippines. As the British had no way of getting reinforcements into Malaya and Singapore as the Japanese forces over-ran those colonies, similarly the United States did not have the resources to reinforce the Philippines. The relocation of the 4th Marines from Shanghai to the Philippines would be a holding operation as there was no way of getting an advantage over the overwhelming number of Japanese who were landing there. These brave American troops, along with the forces of the Philippine Army fought an heroic but futile campaign.

A Senior Archivist at the Marine Corps Research Center in Quantico, Virginia, J Michael Miller, authored a comprehensive 44-page pamphlet entitled: 'From Shanghai to Corregidor: Marines in Defense of the Philippines'. This publication provides in great detail the departure of the 4th Marines from Shanghai and through their subsequent experience in the Philippines, which resulted in the eventual surrender of those islands. After holding out since the initial landing of the Japanese forces on December 8, 1941, General Jonathan Wainwright, Commander of all US forces in the Philippines, decided to surrender at 1200 on May 8, 1942. This, of course, included the 4th Marines.

Mr Miller's pamphlet captures the emotion of the moment: *'At 1200 the white flag came out of the tunnel and Major Williams ordered his men to withdraw to the tunnel and turn in their weapons. The end had come for the 4th Marines. Colonel Curtis ordered Captain Robert B. Moore to burn the 4th Marine Regiment colors. Captain Moore took the colors in his hand and left the headquarters. On return, with tears in his eyes, he reported that the burning had been carried out. Colonel Howard placed his face in his hands and wept, saying, "My God, and I had to be the first Marine officer ever to surrender a regiment".'*

It was decided in February 1944 that the 4th Marine Regiment was to be re-established without colors until earned once again in combat. It seemed fitting that the main components of the regiment would be the four Raider Battalions, which had been operating with valor in the Pacific Theater for the previous couple of years. Each of the four Raider Battalions had served with distinction in several 'raids' and extraordinary combat missions in the early stages of the US mission to defeat the Empire of Japan.

The 4th Marine Regiment became part of the 1st Provisional Marine Brigade, which was assigned to the III Amphibious Corps and won its colors back during the liberation of Guam. It later became part of the 6th Marine Division, which also came under the command of the newly formed III Amphibious Corps.

CHAPTER SIX

HI JINKS ON GUADALCANAL

Guadalcanal, in the Solomon Islands, introduced a new element into my life as a Marine – I became involved in a bit of commerce. Some enterprising young men were making necklaces out of seashells. Cat's Eyes- the opercula of turban shells – were the prettiest and most popular. They would comb the beaches and collect as many as they could find, clean them up (with a quick dunking in spirits of salts, otherwise known as hydrochloric acid), purchase plain silver chains and make the necklaces. The going price was around $30 and they sold pretty well as gifts for sisters, moms, wives and girlfriends back home. One lucrative market was among the young junior officers. Some of us, including yours truly, thought up a way to enter into the trading business.

I had found it worthwhile to become pals with the young officers and spent a fair amount of leisure time with them. My motivation was a craving for knowledge – because of my need to get employment at an early age I lacked a formal education. All the young officers were well educated and we hung around together, having a few drinks and playing poker and blackjack while I fired a series of questions at them about virtually everything. I got away with this by applying simple logic. Off duty these officers were Eddie, Jack, Tom, etc. During duty time I addressed them as Lieutenant so-and-so as appropriate to military protocol. By maintaining the dignity of their office while at work I was allowed to be pals with them when off-duty.

The benefits of our socializing were not only to my advantage – the young officers quickly recognized that I could be useful on a number of levels. Frequently I found myself as a go-between for purchases of items that were crafted by the troops. Enlisted men could, from time to time, buy small quantities of beer from the PX but could not access other alcohol. I would sometimes intervene by offering to acquire necklaces and other goods made by the enlisted men and trade them with my junior officer friends for booze. Officers were permitted to purchase a specified amount of whiskey from the PX at a cost of 50 cents per bottle for most brands and 75 cents for Canadian Club and Scotch. I would sell the whiskey on the open market for about $30 a bottle. I chose not to take advantage of my friendship with the officers. I should make it clear that this kind of trading was done amongst young junior officers who were close to the same age as the enlisted troops. Most of the trading was done with lieutenants and, once in a while, a captain, but never above that level.

One senior officer I befriended, a major, concocted a scheme in which I was to play a role. Female companionship was virtually non-existent – the only eligible females were a few nurses attached to the field hospitals. The major, however, figured out a clever way to get a date once in a while.

On rare occasions an entertainment troupe would visit the island to cheer up the troops. The game we played was pretty cute. The only car in our organization belonged to the Commanding General. The Major would get clearance to use that car and driver to escort the entertainers between where they were staying and their performance venue. The single automobile was too small to transport all of them – up to five men and five women – so we would commandeer a personnel carrier, which I drove.

During the performances we would position the vehicles right off the stage and, at the end of the performances, as the visitors came down the steps, the major and one of his buddies would steer the women into the car while I would steer the men into my vehicle. The car would set off first over the single-track road – with occasional side roads – and I would follow, knowing quite well where the car was headed.

The Officers' Club at Henderson Field on Guadalcanal was the most up-to-date place for entertaining guests and it was on one of the side roads. Shortly before we approached the turn-off point I would find a desperate need to relieve myself so I would announce my intention and pull off to the side of the road, assuring my passengers (who were not pleased with the way things were going) that I would catch up to the car in no time. Surprise, surprise, I never did. Instead I would find myself back at the camp where the entertainers were billeted. I would declare that the car would be along shortly and that I had to leave to get my vehicle back to the motor pool. My unhappy male passengers were helpless but resigned themselves to the fact they had been tricked.

The major and I never discussed anything about these events but I judged his assessment of the evening on how much whiskey he gave me afterwards. One bottle was for doing my duty; a second bottle was probably related to his enjoyment level.

On one occasion I was planning a party for my friends and preferred beer to whiskey because it was easier to control. I typed an official memo to the PX officer, which requested him to sell me two cases of beer – presumably for the major's personal use. I presented it to the major to sign. He looked at it, thought the quantity excessive and tore it up. I responded by preparing subsequent memos, increasing the

53

amount by one case each time. He tore up each request. The game went on until it reached five cases. Exasperated, but in remembrance of the team effort we played on other occasions, he signed the memo.

Anywhere you find Marines there is bound to be a Navy Seabee unit in the vicinity. These guys have great earthmoving capabilities and seem to have everything in the way of tools and equipment, including refrigeration. That means that in the tropics they have ice. For a reasonable amount of beer I acquired all the ice that was needed. With so much treasure on hand and no means for storage, we simply invited almost anyone around into our tent to share our good fortune – with the provision that no unopened cans of beer were to leave the tent.

For the most part I kept my bargaining to a minimum. Perhaps a restraining factor was one time when I negotiated to purchase a case of a dozen bottles of whiskey from an Air Force barber who was stationed at Henderson Field. He managed to secure supplies of booze – I am not sure from where, but suspect it was through quid-pro-quo deals with pilots who regularly flew return trips to Australia.

We made the arrangements: I paid him the agreed amount, loaded the case in my Jeep and drove back to my quarters. The case was unmarked but I was given to understand that it was a US product. Upon opening the case I found it to be an Australian product with which I was unfamiliar. I drove back to the barber and complained. His response was something like: 'caveat emptor – buyer beware' which triggered my anger. So furious was I that I prevailed upon a lieutenant, one of my junior officer friends, to put on a cartridge belt with a .45 caliber pistol attached, thereby creating the impression of police authority. We drove back to the barbershop. The lieutenant ordered me to put the case of whiskey on the floor then turned to the barber and suggested that he return my money, which, of course, he did. On the way back to camp I received a scolding on the inappropriateness of my behaviour and the untenable position in which I had placed my friend. He was right. My anger had pushed me over the top and I was ashamed.

CHAPTER SEVEN

THE MARIANAS CAMPAIGN

In the Solomon Islands we were a long way from the Japanese homeland. Throughout a series of high-level international military conferences in 1943 various ideas for speeding up the Pacific war were presented and discussed.

Admiral Ernest J King, Commander-in-Chief, United States Fleet, championed a plan to throw the power of the Navy behind a drive through the central Pacific. Consistently he presented the Marianas to the Joint Chiefs of Staff (JCS) as a key objective. He felt it was necessary to have these islands to control the central Pacific routes of advances to the Philippines and the Japanese home islands. During JCS conferences in mid-November the Admiral's plan gained a powerful advocate - General Henry H (Hap) Arnold, Commander General, Army Air Forces. Air Force planners felt the B-29 fields that existed in China would not be adequate for the projected air war of attrition against Japan. Proposed bases at Chengtu in Sichuan Province and Chungking would require the big planes either to refuel at supplemental bases or carry a reduced bomb load. Airstrips closer to the China coast could not be considered because the Japanese were either threatening to, or had, captured them. General Arnold felt that the Marianas would offer base security and, at the same time, reduce the round-trip flight for his bombers to Japan by 1200 miles. These factors added to Admiral King's concept - tipping the scale in favor of the central Pacific route.

The Fifth Amphibious Corps (VAC) consisting of the 2nd and 4th Marine Divisions and the Army's XX1V Corps artillery was under the command of Lieutenant General Holland M Smith whose task was to seize Saipan and Tinian.

The Third Amphibious Corps (IIIAC) consisting of the 3rd Marine Division, the 1st Provisional Marine Brigade and the IIIAC Corps Artillery as well as the Army's 77th Infantry Division was under the command of Major General Roy S Geiger whose task was to re-capture Guam.

As the US forces approached confrontation with an unknown enemy, it was essential to understand the workings of the mind and the attitude of the Japanese soldier. An extremely valuable insight was obtained through the capture of Japanese orders and landing instructions prepared by the Japanese early in 1942 for the assault on Midway, Guadalcanal and Makin Island.

The Japanese method of fighting has been described as similar to Jiu Jitsu. Surprise was their ultimate weapon and to deliver their devastating blows they depended on meticulous training, small forces, rapid movement and hand-to-hand fighting.

Training, morale and iron discipline underpinned the Japanese war effort - along with the Japanese culture which incorporated emperor worship. They felt that their cause was holy; they had absolute confidence in the belief that Japanese people were superior to any other race on earth and they had complete confidence in the infallibility of their fighting skills. This combined with the natural gritty determination of their race and the lack of creativity beyond the needs of the task at hand made them a formidable foe.

Not only was the Japanese training exceedingly thorough, but also their methods had been tested and constantly practiced in the war against China.

They also had a fatalistic point of view and would fight to the bitter end. Capture was the same as death because the family of a Japanese serviceman taken prisoner would consider him dead and observe all the rituals following a death. If he returned he would be considered a 'non-person' with all his civil rights gone. Hence the blood-curdling tradition of the kamikaze pilots who left their home bases with only enough fuel for the outward journey. They knew and totally accepted that they were on a suicide mission.

Of the Islands known as the Marianas, Guam is the largest - 30 miles long and nine miles wide. It had been a United States possession since its capture from Spain in 1898. The Japanese captured it on December 10, 1941, following the attack on Pearl Harbor. It was not as heavily fortified as the other Mariana Islands - such as Saipan that had been a Japanese possession since the end of World War I - but by 1944 it had a large Japanese garrison.

Following Admiral King and General Arnold's plan, we boarded the troop ships for the long journey to the Marianas. The trip was to be much longer than we had anticipated because the Japanese fleet came out in force while we were at sea. Our military commanders elected to send the troop ships to the Marshall Islands while our Navy engaged the enemy. Our ship, along with several others, was to anchor off the coast of Kwajalein Atoll. While there, we were allowed to swim in the warm Pacific Ocean and even to go ashore for a few hours. The best thing I can say about shore leave on Kwajalein is that we were off the ship for a few hours to wander around the sand spit with nothing but coconut palm trees. I do not recall how long we were there but it was long enough for our Navy's Task Force 58 to do significant damage to the Japanese Navy in what was termed 'The Battle of the Philippine Sea'. After our Navy had finished with the Japanese fleet and sent the miserable remnants scurrying for safer seas, the threat was removed so we weighed anchors and sailed to our much-anticipated destination.

Liberation Day for Guam began at 0530, July 21, 1944. The US fleet of six battleships, nine cruisers, a host of destroyers and rocket ships attacked the west side of the island with a two-hour bombardment, laying their wrath on the enemy-riddled rice paddies, wrinkled black hills, cliffs and caves.

The Marines had risen at 0230 and eaten their pre-landing breakfast of steak and eggs - which had become a tradition. The assault troops laden with fighting gear, their sheathed bayonets protruding from their packs, bustled about and waited while loudspeakers shouted: 'Now hear this…now hear this…'. Unit commanders visited each of their men, checking gear, straightening packs, rendering an encouraging pat on the shoulder and squaring away the queues before going below to the well decks to board the Landing Vehicles, Tracked (LVTs).

Aircraft roared in over mast tops and naval guns produced a continuous booming background noise. Climaxing it all, from a bulkhead speaker came the voice of General Geiger, Commanding General of the III Amphibious Corps: '*You have been honored. The eyes of the nation watch you as you go into battle to liberate a former American bastion from the enemy. The honor, which has been bestowed on you, is a signal one. May the glorious traditions of the Marine Corps' esprit de corps spur you to victory. You have been honored.'*

The 3rd Marine Division landed near Agana and the 1st Provisional Marine Brigade landed near Agat. By 0900 men and tanks were ashore at both beaches. The 77th Infantry Division followed the 1st Provisional Marine Brigade in at Agat. The men stationed at both beachheads were pinned down by vicious Japanese fire, making initial progress inland quite slow. By nightfall, however, we had managed to push the Japanese 2000 meters – more than a mile - inland.

We at Corps Headquarters landed at Agat two days after the first combat troops and spent the first night in foxholes - but established a command post the following day.

Before leaving Guadalcanal, as we prepared for our first combat mission, Colonel Gale T Cumming's Jeep driver was transferred so I asked the Colonel if he would allow me to take his job. He readily agreed. The relationship that I formed with him is one that I treasured.

Colonel Cummings had a degree in law but had not practiced law in civilian life. He enlisted in the Marine Corps in 1917 and was now in the twilight of his career. Having responsibility for personnel operations of the Corps was a match of talent. He was an extremely practical person and a brilliant strategist, as well as having a heart of gold. His compassion for his fellow man had no bounds. He seemed to always be in touch with what was going on, not only in the G-1 Section, but also in the whole Corps. When in the rear areas, life was easy. When we were in the forward areas, he maintained a complete awareness of where the battles were taking place and a command of the topography of the entire island. This was essential, as we were often required to visit the front lines and, sometimes, even penetrate behind enemy lines. Going behind enemy lines was not in his job description but since he had responsibility for determining locations of future command posts and supply depots, he was ready and keen to reach a little further. He always maintained a map of the island we were on in his office and through his various contacts, knew exactly where the action was taking place.

Normally when we visited the front line units, it was just the Colonel and me but when we ventured into territory behind the lines of battle, Lieutenant Eddie Coontz, the Colonel's aide and Corporal Nick Breen, his orderly would ride shotgun in the back seat- just in case. Fortunately, we never needed to engage the enemy ourselves.

Eddie Coontz and Nick Breen had been with Colonel Cummings from when the 1st Marine Amphibious Corps departed the United States. A more dedicated and loyal pair of Marines did not exist. Often, using the authority of the Colonel, Lieutenant Coontz acted on his behalf - many times without the knowledge of the Colonel. As for Nick Breen, he loved the Colonel as much as he did his New York City Irish father and looked after his needs and items of comfort with tender care. When we were in our headquarters locations we had access to laundry facilities but when we were engaged in combat campaigns, such luxuries were not available. We did, however, sleep on canvas cots most of the time, with thin mattresses. While in combat zones Nick did the Colonel's laundry by hand and folded and placed his shirts and trousers under his mattress - which took the place of an iron which, of course, we did not have. Other officers wondered why Colonel Cummings always dressed so well.

One time while we were visiting front line units, we happened to be in a village, which our troops had just captured. In his inimitable fashion, Colonel Cummings talked to the village leaders and asked if there was anything they needed. The Village Chief told him that there were two small girls who had high fevers and he was concerned over their health. Colonel Cummings said that we would take them to one of our field hospitals and care for them and bring them back when they were well. I carried one of the girls and one of a film crew from our Public Relations section, which was filming events, carried the other girl to our Jeep and into the care of Eddie Coontz and Nick Breen. The camera crew photographed the scene, and the footage made it into the syndicated news.

In US movie theaters in those days - prior to television - it was customary to show news items before the feature film under the title (with appropriate music and drum-rolls): Movietone News. My father, who was serving as a butcher in the US Army Air Corps in New Haven Connecticut, saw the story about the rescue and treatment of the two feverish girls and made a scene when he saw his son on the screen. The theater manager calmed him down and took him to the projection booth. They went through the scenes off-line and he had the projectionist cut out a couple of frames and gave them to my father. Eventually, it was featured in the newspapers and distributed to all members of our family.

An incident occurred while I was on Guam that, completely unknown to me could have far-reaching implications and would have, without staunch friends in positions of command, wreaked havoc on my career as a Marine. Being an election year, Washington had dispatched a lieutenant colonel to Guam to supervise and encourage Marines to participate in the general election. Ever willing to help anyone in need, Colonel Cummings offered me as a driver to take the visitor wherever he needed to go in the performance of his duties. Much of this was to front line units. One day as I was making preparations to take the

Lieutenant Colonel to the front lines, Colonel Cummings called me into the office where he kept a huge map which was constantly updated with a plethora of information including who controlled what territory - our forces or the Japanese. He pointed to the location of the front line units we were to visit and the route we were to take to get there. Then he directed me to me another section and pointed out a road behind enemy lines that appeared to be much shorter and a possible route for our return. The G-3 Section, which managed operations, advised us that it was estimated we would push the Japanese across that road but that would not be until the following day. Therefore, Colonel Cummings suggested that I might want to take a look at the situation and (as we had done in the past) if it looked viable, that I would choose that route.

When I approached the road in question, it looked solid and there was no sign of action, so I took that track. The entire length we were to traverse was about five miles and it all looked in order.

Everything went smoothly for about three miles and then we heard the sounds of small arms fire from the direction of our lines. While I accelerated I advised my passenger to take my rifle out of its holder and be prepared, 'just in case' as I was going to put my foot to the floorboard and get out of there as quickly as possible.

A short distance later, the gunfire appeared closer but behind us. We paused momentarily, looked back in the direction from whence we came and saw Japanese soldiers falling back across the road. I was confident that we were out of danger. My passenger demanded to know: 'what the hell is going on?' As we drove on I explained to him the strategy Colonel Cummings and I had devised early that morning. He was not happy and when we arrived back at our Command Post, he charged into our office and screamed at Colonel Cummings, that I almost got him killed. In his normal, cool manner, Colonel Cummings simply said that there was no need for further concern as henceforth, the visiting lieutenant colonel could requisition a vehicle from the motor pool and find someone to drive for him, as I was no longer available. This lieutenant colonel - let's call him 'Scrooge' - then directed his ire at me and apparently stowed this incident away in his memory files marked 'N' for Nasty and 'R' for Retribution. Of course I was totally oblivious to all this. I had simply been doing my job.

The counterattacks against the American beachhead, as well as the fierce fighting, had exhausted the Japanese. At the start of August, they were running out of food and ammunition and had only a handful of tanks left. Lieutenant General Takeshi Takashima, the Japanese Commanding General, had been killed on July 28 and his second-in-command, Lieutenant Hideyoshi Obata took over, leading the remaining defense forces.

General Obata withdrew his troops from the south of Guam, planning to make a stand in the mountainous central and northern part of the island. With re-supply and reinforcement impossible because of the American control of the sea and air around Guam, he could hope to do no more than delay the inevitable defeat for a few days.

Rain and thick jungle made conditions difficult for our troops, but after an engagement at Mount Barrigard from August 2 to 4, the Japanese line collapsed; the rest of the battle was a pursuit to the north. As in other battles of the Pacific War, the Japanese refused to surrender and almost all were killed. On August 10, after three long weeks of bloody and ferocious fighting, organized Japanese resistance ended and Guam was declared secure. The next day General Obata committed ritual suicide.

A final note having to do with personal responsibility and morality: one day I went to the PX to buy cigarettes. It was pay day, so big bills were on hand. The two Marines in front of me each bought 2 cartons of cigarettes and paid for them with a $20.00 bill (fifty cents a carton). I also bought two cartons but paid with a $10.00 bill. The clerk having established a routine with the two former customers gave me change for $20.00 instead of $10.00. At first I felt like I hit a lottery and was delighted. My ever present conscience however got into the act. What was I to do? Not comfortable with returning to the PX because of the waiting time involved, I decided on alternative action. There was a chapel nearby so I drove over there and put the $10.00 bill in the poor box. My soul was cleansed.

In the Battle for control of the Marianas Islands, Saipan was the first, followed shortly thereafter by the battles for Tinian and then Guam. Three weeks into the battle for Saipan, there was no doubt about the outcome of the V Amphibious Corps and commanders began turning their attention to the next objective - the island of Tinian, visible three miles off Saipan's southern coast. Tinian was important because, although it is a plateau rising up from the sea, unlike Saipan, its terrain is flat and ideal for our long-range bombers.

In retrospect, after the war, Admiral Spruance expressed the opinion: 'The Tinian operation was probably the most brilliantly conceived and executed amphibious operation of the Pacific War'. The Commanding General of the V Amphibious Corps, General Holland Smith was more specific: 'Tinian was the perfect amphibious operation in the Pacific War'.

To my mind, the brilliance and tenacity of General Smith and the heroic and intelligent analysis of a very dear friend of mine were contributing factors.

In planning the operation, the crucial question of where they were to land was undecided. There was strong support among the planners for a landing on two narrow sand strips - code named White Beach1 and White Beach 2 on Tinian's northwest coast. Vice-Admiral Richard Turner, overall Commander of the Marianas Expeditionary Force, however, was skeptical. He leaned toward Yellow Beach, made up of several wide, sandy strips in front of Tinian Town, the island's heavily fortified administrative and commercial center. There were heated exchanges between Admiral Turner and General Holland Smith over this issue.

The V Amphibious Corps Amphibious Reconnaissance Battalion, commanded by Captain James L Jones, was put on alert for reconnaissance of these potential landing sites. On July 9 Jones got his orders from Lieutenant General Holland Smith. His men were to scout out the Tinian beaches and their fortifications and their capacity to handle the landing force and keep it supplied. The rest of this story is told in the words of Lieutenant Theodore Toole, USMCR.

'Our teams were to investigate and secure accurate information concerning the height and nature of the reef

shelf, depth of water, location and nature of mines and underwater obstacles, the slope of the bottom of the beaches, the height and nature of cliffs flanking and behind the beaches, exits for vehicles, and the nature of vegetation behind the beaches. "A" Company was to scout out Yellow Beach 1 while "B" Company was assigned to the White Beaches.

'On the evening of July 10th, we boarded two navy destroyer transport vessels, the Gilmer and the Stringham and proceeded to their respective stations off Yellow Beach 1 and the White beaches.

'One of the destroyers took a team to within 3000 yards of Yellow Beach 1 and lowered rubber boats from the low end of the stern section into the water. They rowed to within 500 yards of the beach, left the rubber boats and swam the rest of the way. They found Yellow Beach to be heavily guarded by anti-vehicle equipment, many floating mines in the water, double apron barbed wire strung along the beach, Japanese sentries on a cliff overlooking the beach and occasional searchlights scanning the beach. Nearby Japanese work crews were building pillboxes and trenching, as they no doubt anticipated our landing to be here. Clearly a landing on this beach would be unfavorable. With this knowledge, the teams made it back to the destroyer.

'Meanwhile, on the other side of the island, the reconnaissance of White Beaches 1 and 2 hit a snag. As our rubber boats were cast off from the destroyer they were

70

swept rapidly to the north by a strong current. The team headed for White Beach 1 never made it ashore. My team which was headed for White Beach 2, ended up on White Beach 1, which left White Beach 2 un-reconnoitered. The Gilmer picked up both parties and took us back to Saipan.

The next night, our Company was assigned to get into both White beaches with 5 two-man teams. With me was a young Corporal and our mission was to scout out White Beach 2. The destroyer took us to within 3000 yards of the beach and dropped us off in rubber boats. We paddled to within 1500 yards, and then swam the rest of the way in. We discovered that there were only two machine guns on the beach and it did not seem to be heavily guarded.

Although the beach itself was only 300 yards wide, there was a coral shelf, which was 900 yards wide, which was sufficient for a regiment to land with troops and vehicles. There were no mines in the water. Having made our discovery, we swam back out to sea. Unfortunately, the rubber boats were gone so we continued to swim toward Saipan in the hopes of finding one of the destroyers. We were in the water for about eight hours when one of the destroyers spotted us and picked us up. They told us that they had been looking for us. They gave us dry clothes and proceeded to Saipan. As soon as we got ashore, I was hustled into a Jeep and rushed to Admiral Turner's headquarters and ushered into a tent full of Admirals, Generals and Colonels. Although dog tired, I was overwhelmed by the presence of so much rank. General Holland Smith asked me to describe what we found out and what my recommendation was. I reported what had been seen at Yellow Beach 1 the previous day and what we discovered on White Beach 2. With this information and the reports from White Beach 1, General Smith declared that we were going to land on the White Beaches. Having heard our reports, Admiral Turner, withdrew his previous objections. Admiral Spuance, who was Admiral Turner's superior gave the final approval to land on the White Beaches

There is no doubt that a landing at Tinian Town (Yellow Beach 1) would have been a disaster and the loss of lives and equipment would have been devastating. General Smith was well aware of that and for his service, Lieutenant Toole was awarded the Silver Star.

The victory over the Marianas islands led the way for our heavy bombers to pound the home islands of Japan with ferocity, and expedited the next major operation, which was the retaking of the Philippines. The Enola Gay took off from Tinian in August carrying the first atomic bomb to be dropped on Japan.

The III Amphibious Corps established Guam as the new base of operations and began to prepare for the next mission which was the attack on the southernmost islands of Japan in the Ryukyu Islands and would be the largest amphibious assault in the Pacific of World War II.

CHAPTER EIGHT

OTHER PACIFIC THEATER ACTION

While we were making preparations for the next major offensive of the III Amphibious Corps, there was a lot of other action going on in the Pacific. As part of the Marianas and Palau Islands campaign, code named Operation Forager, we had completed the Marianas part, having conquered Saipan, Guam and Tinian. The remaining portion of that campaign was the assault on Peleliu, where 11,000 Japanese military personnel and Korean and Okinawan laborers prepared for a new island defense strategy. Under the Command of Colonel Kunio Nakagawa, they chose to abandon the old tactic of stopping the enemy at the beach. The new strategy was to use the rough terrain to their advantage, by constructing a system of heavily fortified bunkers, caves and underground positions all interlocked into a 'honeycomb' system. The old tactic of the banzai charge - Japanese human wave attacks mounted by infantry units crying 'Tenno Heika Banzai' (long live the emperor) was discontinued as wasteful of men and ineffective. It was one of Japan's least-effective strategies in terms of Japanese-American casualty ratios.

The neutralization of Peleliu and the sister island of Angaur, was essential to protect MacArthur's right flank as he was preparing for the return to the Philippines. After a hard fought two-month battle, our forces finally prevailed by November 27, 1944, having experienced the highest casualty rate for US military personnel of any battle in the Pacific war so far.

Upon Admiral Halsey's recommendation, the Combined Chiefs of Staff approved the decision to move up the date of the first landing in the Philippines, which was to begin at the central Philippine island of Leyte. The new date set for the landing on Leyte, October 1944 was two months before the previous target date to land on Mindanao in the southern Philippines.

General Douglas MacArthur fulfilled his promise to the Filipino people as the assault on the Philippines began in October 1944. The Filipinos were ready and waiting for the invasion. It would be eight long and bloody months until the final Japanese resistance ended in that country. In November 1944, the US Navy began the bombardment of Iwo Jima. Iwo was strategically important for the Japanese as it provided an air base for Japanese fighter planes to intercept our long-range B-29 Super Fortress bombers on their way to the main Japanese islands, and it provided a haven for Japanese naval units in dire need of any support available. In addition, it was used by the Japanese to stage air attacks on the Marianas Islands. Iwo Jima also served as an early warning station that radioed reports of incoming bombers back to mainland Japan.

It was equally strategically important to us as well. With three airfields, it would provide facilities for our P-51 Mustang fighter planes to escort our heavy bombers coming from the Marianas, on their way to bomb the Japanese homeland. It would also serve as an emergency landing place for our long-range planes, which may be low on fuel or had been hit while on their bombing missions.

Lieutenant General Tadamichi Kuribayashi was assigned to command the defense of Iwo Jima in June 1944. He knew that Japan could not win the battle, but he hoped to inflict massive casualties on the American Forces, so that the United States and its Australian and British Allies would reconsider carrying out the impending invasion of Japan.

By drawing inspiration from the defense in the Battle of Peleliu, Kuribayashi designed a defense that broke with Japanese military doctrine. Rather than establishing his defenses on the beach to face the landings directly, he created strong, mutually supporting defensives in depth using static and heavy weapons. Because the tunnel linking the mountain to the main forces was never completed, Kuribayashi organized the southern area of the island in and around Mount Suribachi as a semi-independent sector, with his main defensive zone built up in the north. The expected American naval and air bombardment further prompted the creation of an extensive system of tunnels that connected the prepared positions, so that a pillbox that had been cleared could be reoccupied. The network of bunkers and pillboxes favored the defense.

(In the war in the Pacific the Japanese constructed pillboxes wherever there was time and adequate materials. Their preferred pillbox was well-camouflaged with thick reinforced concrete walls and roof and narrow firing slits that allowed the occupants to fire on approaching troops while severely restricting their personal exposure.)

The Marines nevertheless found ways to prevail under the circumstances, although the Iwo Jima campaign took a heavy toll on Americans as well as Japanese. The 36-day assault resulted in more than 26,000 American casualties, including 6800 dead. Of the 22,000 Japanese soldiers entrenched on the island, 21,844 died, and only 216 were captured. Although the number of Japanese killed was three times that of the Americans, this was the only battle by the US Marine Corps in which the overall American casualties exceeded those of the Japanese. The island was declared secured on March 26 1945.

CHAPTER NINE

THE OKINAWA CAMPAIGN

In the planning for our next operation, some of us 'grunts' who served high ranking officers were involved more in this phase than we had been previously, which was a compliment we took seriously and therefore respected the newly-placed level of responsibility. We learned that our next landing would be on Okinawa although we had no inkling of the timing.

Many other events contributed to the neglect of Okinawa in the public memory of World War II. The bloody battle of Iwo Jima was fresh on the minds of Americans, the war in Europe was front-page news, the Soviet Union declared war on Japan five days after our landing and President Roosevelt died one week later.

Operation Iceberg, the code name, was fought on the 30 Ryukyu Islands of Okinawa and was the largest amphibious assault in the Pacific War. The 82-day long battle lasted from early April until mid-June of 1945. After a long campaign of island hopping, the allies were approaching the Japanese homeland.

More people died during the battle of Okinawa than all of those killed in the atomic bombings of Hiroshima and Nagasaki. This proved to be the bloodiest battle of the Pacific War. Casualties totaled more than 38,000 Americans wounded and 12,000 killed. More than 107,000 Japanese and Okinawan conscripts were killed plus another 24,000 sealed in caves or buried by the Japanese themselves. Over 10,000 were captured or surrendered. More than 100,000 Okinawan civilians perished in the battle. No battle during World War II, except Stalingrad, had as massive a loss of civilian life. A total of 36 Allied ships and other craft of all types had been sunk (mostly by Kamikazes) and 368 ships and other craft damaged. The fleet lost 763 aircraft. In contrast, the Japanese lost 7,380 aircraft and 16 combat ships. Several high-ranking sources speculated that the cost of this battle in terms of Allied lives lost, weighed heavily in the decision to use the atomic bomb against the Japanese.

The Japanese were well aware that they could not prevail against the might of the combined forces of the United States, the United Kingdom, Canada, Australia and New Zealand so their mission became a battle of attrition. For every Japanese soldier lost, the remaining men were ordered to kill ten Americans, or members of the Allied forces. For every Japanese aircraft lost they were ordered to sink a ship or some other naval craft. The objective was to destroy, or at worst, delay the US fleet. It was reasoned that this would give them more time to prepare for the defense of the homeland. Lieutenant General Mitsuri Ushijima would have more than 110,000 men, which included the Okinawan Home Guard and even middle school senior boys under his command.

The Japanese did not view Okinawans to be on the same level as themselves and used them (or abused them) as pieces, in a game of 'Go' - as often referred to by the former Okinawan Governor, Masahide Ota. (Go is an ancient board game played in Asia.) Alternately, they were described as being 'caught between the hammer and the anvil'. The Okinawans were docile people, of small stature, and were in an unenviable situation. The Japanese had brainwashed them to believe that the Americans were barbarians who would rape their women and eat their children. The value of propaganda was well recognized and used by the Japanese.

For the Allies, the battle of Okinawa was an important part of the US Pacific military strategy, which was to strike right into the industrial heart of Japan.

In mid-March, 1945, the American fleet of 1300 ships under the command of Admiral Spruance gathered off the cost of Okinawa for the naval bombardment. Included in the armada were several Pearl Harbor survivors as well as the

British Carrier force TF-57 with four aircraft carriers, two battleships, and 14 destroyers.

On April 1 (Easter Sunday), designated 'L' Day, under the overall command of Lieutenant General Simon Bolivar Buckner, the Tenth Army made its landings. For this operation, the Tenth Army included Army XXIV Corps consisting of the 7th and 96th Infantry Divisions and the 1st and 6th Divisions of the Marine III Amphibious Corps. The 2nd Marine Division was held in reserve as well as the Army 27th Division and the 77th Infantry Division. At the start of the battle, General Buckner had more than 182,000 Army, Navy and Marine Corps troops under his command.

The Japanese chose not to defend the beaches as part of their overall strategy to avoid casualties against the overwhelming Allied firepower; therefore both the Army and Marine Corps landings were uncontested. We walked ashore and drove across the island, the Marines to the northern sector and the Army to the southern sector.

In contrast to my going ashore on Guam on the second day of the battle, on Okinawa, I was in the third wave. We quickly advanced inland and occupied Kadena Air Base by noon. On the first night ashore, we experienced incoming shellfire as we were hunkered down behind walls of abandoned buildings. We were reminded that as long as we could hear the whistle of the shells, it meant they had passed our location. When the whistling stopped we knew it would be followed by an explosion - too close for comfort. When that happened we hugged the walls and tried to get under something solid while all hell broke loose around us.

The battle plan called for the Marines to head north while the Army divisions were to head south. There were good reasons for attacking northward without delay. The sooner this was done, the less chance the enemy would have to organize and fortify their forces and positions. Colonel Udo, Commander of the Japanese forces in the north, was known to be organizing the Okinawans for guerilla warfare. There was also the threat of counter landings in the small ports of northern Okinawa by Japanese moving in from other Ryukyu Islands or from Japan itself. By securing the ports this threat could be removed.

By the afternoon of April 4, the 6th Marine Division was moving off the high coral cliffs that overlook Ishikawa Isthmus, the narrow waist of the island leading off to the north, and advanced to the long beach that faces the sea at the town of Ishikawa on the east coast.

North of the Nakadomari-Ishikawa line scattered groups of Japanese were straggling toward Motobu Peninsula; south of it American tanks were moving up to assembly areas while engineers were organizing supply dumps and bulldozing wide roads. This rear area work by the engineers was vital for the advance northward. The Divisions' hardest task was to move troops, vehicles, supplies, tanks, and guns over the one-way roads without losing the momentum that had been moving at the rate of 7000 yards a day. The 22nd Marines and the 4th Marines devised a method of leapfrogging that freed roads and provided security. Enemy resistance continued to be spasmodic and was usually dispatched quickly.

Reconnaissance units and tanks of the 29th Marines advanced into Nago, a medium-sized town nestling in the deep bend where Motobu juts out westward from the island. A spearhead drove north to Tiara, cutting the Motobu Peninsula off from the rest of Okinawa.

Here, for the first time, we were meeting not stragglers but outposts of an organized defense and became involved in fire fights and had to deal with organized rifle fire. Motobu Peninsula was largely unknown territory to the Americans as much of the interior was cloud-covered when the first photographs were taken and failed to disclose important trails hidden under the trees; it was only after a Japanese map had been captured that the complete road network was made clear.

We found the peninsula to be virtually a country in itself, inhabited by mountain farmers who dug out their plots on steep slopes. The Japanese were well prepared for mountain warfare. The rugged landscape and the knowledge of the area proved to be a distinct advantage. They knew the trails and they had horses, the best means of transportation over this terrain. Though the forces in the north were generally weak in equipment and supplies, the best of what was available had been concentrated in Motobu. They were especially strong in automatic weapons, among them were 25mm naval guns set in emplacements in the masses of hill. With mortars and machine guns that were easily carried, as well as fixed 25mm guns and at least a battery of field artillery, Colonel Udo might well have hoped to maintain control of this mountain stronghold for a considerable time.

Because of the rugged terrain up the ridges and the narrow valleys, our infantry had to depend on its organic weapons; artillery and air strikes were more effective when the heights were taken, but tanks were out of the question.

The rapid advance strained every resource of the shore parties so Nago became the site of the division command post and was now the nerve center; supplies were being brought to its harbor by LVTs as the long road haul over the isthmus had been largely abandoned. Control of the roads south of Nago was transferred to a very large body of Seabees who were busy reconstructing roads and bridges.

As we moved further into the Motobu Peninsula, we met varying degrees of Japanese resistance. The enemy had good observation of the movement of our Marines so they applied a strategy of allowing a few troops to pass across an open saddle and then firing on the group from behind. American officers were favorite targets. It was dangerous to hold a map, to wave a directing arm, or even show a pistol rather than a rifle or carbine. Under the circumstances, the companies deployed rapidly and on many occasions the approach march became a series of assaults as fire teams engaged with enemy outposts.

The Marines, accustomed to grappling with solid defense lines on small islands, now had to use tactics of manoeuvre 'right out of the book'.

The 4th Marine Regiment had joined in the battle and swung north as the enemy withdrew and on the April 18 the 4th and the 29th Regiments joined ranks in pursuit of the fleeing enemy.

The 6th Division had broken the main enemy defenses north of the landing beaches but enough Japanese remained to participate in organized guerilla warfare. Until the 6th Division moved south in May, the Marines patrolled and reduced enemy pockets in Motobuto and northern Okinawa.

On the final push to the northernmost tip of Okinawa, someone came up with the idea that, temporarily, Corporal

Hook should give up his position behind the wheel of a vehicle and gain some first-hand experience as a foot soldier. I think it might have been at the suggestion of Lieutenant Eddie Coontz, that I joined some patrols in the final push northward. (I think he was driving my Jeep, in which he and Colonel Cummings were following not too far behind).

This gave me a different perspective on war and my respect for the front- lines Marines took a quantum leap. I was in a double line of Marines moving northward - covering both sides the road - when an amusing incident occurred. I was about the 15th person behind the point man, when someone from the rear began shouting: 'they are hitting our flanks'. The message was swiftly relayed up toward the front of the patrol. Upon hearing the warning, some of us swung our rifles off our shoulders and prepared for action. One seasoned Marine near me kept marching, as cool as a cucumber, and yelled: 'What are they hitting us with, rocks?' Having heard no sounds of gunfire, he was not taken in. The sounds of laughter resonated through the ranks. In such a tense situation it was a moment of comic relief that served to release a little of the pressure which we were under.

During this period, the 6th Marine Division had moved 84 miles, seized 436 square miles of enemy territory, counted over 2500 enemy bodies and captured 46 prisoners. Our losses during the period were 436 killed, 1061 wounded, and seven missing. During the rapid advance of the Division from Yonton Airdrome to the northern tip of Okinawa practically every type of action was employed and all types of supply problems encountered.

We established the III Amphibious Corps command post somewhere in that area and operated out of there until we eventually moved to Naha after it fell into our hands.

Having fulfilled our initial mission, our forces joined the 1st Marine Division, which had swung alongside the Army troops and directed our attention to the southern part of the island where the heaviest part of the campaign was being wagered.

Japanese air opposition had been relatively light during the first few days after the landings. However on April 6, the expected air reaction began with an attack by 400 planes from Kyushu. Periodic heavy air attacks continued through April. During the period between March 26 and April 30, 20 American ships were sunk and 157 damaged by enemy action. Up to that period, the Japanese had lost more than 1100 planes in the battle.

At our command post, a loudspeaker was hoisted high in one of the large trees and was connected to a communications unit, which was constantly in touch with air operations, so we had constant reports of the air action.

87

Daily kamikaze attacks were flown from Kyushu and Formosa (currently Taiwan). A mixture of emotions was felt as we listened to the announcements. The raids were designated as bogey (enemy air) raids and they were numbered. Normally there were three planes in each raid. Their primary targets were our ships, which were off the west coast of Okinawa. The first reference point was Point Bolo, which was to the north of Yontan and Kadena Air bases on the west coast.

Announcements went something like this: *'Bogey Raid #1 consisting of three aircraft is X miles west of Point Bolo'.* This would be followed by a report that our fighters were zeroing in on their targets. Shortly thereafter another announcement would be heard to the effect that Bogey Raid #1 has been splashed. We had heard about inexperienced pilots being commanded to fly those planes, which had only enough fuel for the outgoing flight; they were not going home. Vice Admiral C R Brown put it in these words: *'There was a hypnotic fascination to the sight so alien to our Western philosophy. We watched each plunging kamikaze with the detached horror of one witnessing a terrible spectacle rather than as the intended victim. We forgot self for the moment as we groped hopelessly for the thoughts of that other man up there'.*

Since those dreadful days I have often pondered the chasm between Oriental and what we call 'Western' thinking.

88

These days, when we face attacks by terrorists I wonder about the similarities between kamikaze pilots and suicide bombers - both seeking glorification through personal sacrifice.

The fighting in the south was much more fierce than it was in the north as the Japanese had elected to put most of their resources into that sector. The Army was moving slowly and at great cost of lives and resources when the Marines pulled in beside them to continue the attack forward.

From our command post in the north, Colonel Cummings ventured forth to the front line units gathering information on personnel activities and scouting future sights for command posts, supply depots and ammunition dumps. We had ample opportunity to view the movement of our forces as we moved slowly southward. Sometimes we would slip behind enemy lines for quick looks, but did not linger any longer than necessary. Colonel Cummings always had maps and battle plans and his calculations proved to be reliable. We had a couple of close calls but we adhered to his orders - under no circumstances would we leave the Jeep and I was to floorboard the accelerator until we removed ourselves from harm's way. Once in a while, after making such a venture, we would speak to front line commanders and give them information on the terrain. They were astounded.

Colonel Cummings, Lieutenant Coontz, Nick Breen and I had enough adventures together to take these occasional journeys into the unknown in our stride. We were not alone, as other members of our office team made similar trips as well. There is a huge difference between getting close to the action as observers and reporters and in being engaged in the actual fighting day in and day out.

In the relatively safe area of our command post, the mundane work that goes on inside the office can become boring. So it was that on one occasion, Lieutenant Charles Rush was assigned to make a trip to Tenth Army Headquarters with reports on behalf of Colonel Cummings. Naturally I would drive for him on the mission. There was an office clerk, Corporal George, however, who was anxious to get out into the field for a break and he asked me if he could do the driving for Lt Rush. I was unwilling but since Lt Rush was agreeable, we sought the approval of Colonel Cummings. Initially he was reluctant but then gave in. He warned both Lt Rush and Corporal George to exercise caution and not to take unnecessary risks, as there were still pockets of Japanese moving in and out of the territory between our command post and that of the Tenth Army. The Colonel and I both cautioned that if they did not complete their mission well before nightfall, they should spend the night at Tenth Army Headquarters rather than risk the drive back after dark.

Our warnings, however, were not heeded as, upon completing their task close to dusk, they decided to make the two-hour trip back to our headquarters. They were within a few miles of our camp when they were ambushed by a Japanese patrol with a machine gun. Lt Rush was shot in the abdomen and the force of his body caused George to swerve the Jeep into a shallow ditch. Lt Rush jumped out of the jeep and headed for a wooded area. George found refuge underneath the vehicle. Throughout the night he could hear the moans of Lt Rush but was afraid to venture out to try to help him. At daybreak, he heard a vehicle approaching and peeped out from his hiding place to see an American troop carrier passing by. The Japanese had apparently packed up and moved out. George scrambled out from under the vehicle, helped Lt Rush back into the jeep and drove immediately to a field hospital within our command post. The doctors and medical staff worked valiantly to save him but to no avail. Lt Rush did not make it. It was sad as he was a young man and had gotten married just before shipping out of the US. Compassion for George, rather than a reprimand seemed appropriate. I felt a tremendous amount of guilt for allowing someone else to do a job I should have performed and spent most of the day on my knees at the chapel.

The southern part of the island was honeycombed with caves, which the Japanese used effectively in their effort to stifle our advance. They sent civilians out at gunpoint to acquire water and supplies for them, which led to civilian casualties. The American advance was inexorable but at great cost to our forces, the Japanese military and the pitiful Okinawa citizens.

While the 6th Marine Division cleared northern Okinawa, the US Army 96th Infantry Division and the 7th Infantry Division wheeled south across the narrow waist of Okinawa. The 96th Division began to encounter fierce resistance in west-central Okinawa about five miles northwest of Shuri. The 7th Division encountered similarly fierce opposition from a rocky pinnacle, which was southeast of the 96th position.

By the night of April 8, US troops had cleared these and several other strongly fortified positions. The toll was heavy in the process for the Americans - but it cost the Japanese three times as many killed or captured. The battle, however, had only just begun - and it was now realized they were merely outposts guarding the Shuri Line.

The next American objective was Kakazu Ridge, two hills with a connecting saddle that formed part of Shuri's outer defenses. The Japanese had prepared their positions well and fought tenaciously. They knew the terrain well and a network of caves provided the opportunity for them to hit and hide. Consequently the American assault stalled and

General Ushijima took advantage of the situation. He decided to take the offensive. On the evening of April 12· the Japanese 32nd Army attacked US positions across the entire front. Their offensive was heavy, sustained and well organized. After fierce close combat, the attackers retreated, only to repeat their offensive the following night. This effort led the Japanese to believe that the Americans were vulnerable to night infiltration tactics, but our superior firepower made any offensive by concentrations of Japanese troops extremely dangerous. They quickly realized the error of their ways and reverted to their defensive strategy.

The US Army 27th Division landed on April 9 and took over on the right along the west coast of Okinawa. General John R Hodge now had three divisions in the line, with the 96th in the middle, the 7th on the east - each division holding a front of about one-and-a-half miles. He launched a new offensive on the April 19 with a barrage of 324 guns, the largest ever in the Pacific Ocean Theater. Battleships, cruisers and destroyers joined the bombardment, which was followed by 650 Navy and Marine planes attacking the enemy positions with napalm, rockets and machine guns. The Japanese defenses were sited on reverse slopes, where the defenders waited out the artillery barrage and aerial attack in relative safety, emerging from the caves to rain mortar rounds and grenades upon the Americans advancing up the forward slope.

The 2nd Marine Division, which had been held in reserve, created a diversionary feint off the Minatoga beaches which drew the Japanese reserves further south. That action weakened their defenses and, coupled with the tenacity of the US Army troops, achieved a push through the Machinato defensive line.

Sadly, we received news that Ernie Pyle had been killed on the small island of Ie Shima on April 18. Ernie was a war correspondent whose career in journalism began in 1923. After several years travelling the world and writing about people and their experiences, his patriotism persuaded him to go to London in 1940 to report on the London bombings by the Nazis. He then lived with the American troops in Ireland and went into action with them in Africa. From there he travelled to the war front on to the European mainland, often writing his columns and chapters for his book while taking cover in foxholes. It was here that the Pyle legend burst into flower.

At the end of war in Europe he returned to his wife and home in Albuquerque, New Mexico for a short period at home before moving to Hollywood to assist in the development of the film version one of his books. When that was completed he felt compelled to return to the battlefields in the Pacific. On that fateful day in April he was traveling with Colonel Joseph Coolidge, US Army, when they were fired upon by a Japanese machine gun.

They jumped out of the Jeep and dove into a roadside ditch to take cover but it did not provide sufficient protection. Another burst of machine gun fire came and Ernie was killed instantly, the bullet entering his left temple just under his helmet. His remains are enshrined at the National Memorial Cemetery of the Pacific at Punchbowl on the island of Oahu, Hawaii. A stone monument was erected on Ie Shima at the site where Ernie was killed. The monument, a truncated pyramid, is engraved with the words: 'At this spot, the 77th Infantry Division lost a buddy, Ernie Pyle, 18 April, 1945'.

By the end of April, the 1st Marine Division relieved the 27th Army Division and the 77th Army Division relieved the 7th Division. When the 6th Marine Division arrived from their northern action, they took over the right flank and the Tenth Army assumed control of the battle.

On May 4 the Japanese launched another counter offensive. This time, Ushijima attempted to make amphibious assaults on the coasts behind American lines. To support his offensive, the Japanese artillery moved into the open. By doing so, they were able to fire 13,000 rounds, but an effective US counter artillery offensive destroyed dozens of Japanese weapons and the attack failed.

The combined forces under the command of General Buckner launched another major attack on May 11. Ten days of fierce fighting followed. Elements of the Army captured Conical Hill while the Marines captured Sugar Loaf Hill. The capture of these two key positions exposed the Japanese around Shuri on both sides. General Buckner hoped to envelope Shuri and trap the main Japanese defense force.

As if we did not have enough difficulty fighting a belligerent foe, toward the end of May we were confronted with another enemy which further inhibited our progress: the weather. We had been fortunate that the monsoon season was late but now Mother Nature inflicted a serious blow. The almost continual downpour filled the area with mud and water. Tanks were bogged down, helplessly mired. Amphibian tractors were unable to negotiate the morass and the front line units, which depended on these vehicles for carrying supplies forward in bad weather, now had to resort to the hand-carrying of supplies and bringing the wounded back where they could be treated. Litter cases were carried through knee-deep mud.

On our numerous trips, we drove through some difficult areas. Sometimes, the muddy water was so deep that it almost came into the vehicle. I had to drive very slowly so as not to create waves. I depended on the heat of the engine to dry the water being splashed up by the fan belt. Upon getting back to our command post I would take the Jeep to the motor pool to steam clean the engine. I was very fortunate to have such a reliable vehicle. From Guadalcanal, through the Guam and Okinawa campaigns, it served us well.

The living conditions of front-line troops were indescribably bad. Foxholes dug into the clay slopes caved in from the constant soaking and, even when the sides held, they had to be bailed out repeatedly. Clothes and equipment, and the men's bodies were wet for days. The bodies of Japanese killed at night lay outside the foxholes, decomposing under swarms of flies. Sanitation measures broke down. The troops were often hungry. Sleep was almost impossible. The monsoon season was taking an ever-increasing toll on the fighting men.

Under these conditions the Marine attack against Wana Ridge was at a standstill. The action degenerated into what was called in official reports: 'aggressive patrolling'. Enemy mortar and artillery fire continued to play against the American front lines, especially at dusk and at night.

The last week of May pointed up the importance of logistical support to the battle. Mud was seriously interrupting our supply lines. Ammunition, water and food had to be hand carried from the rear for distances as great as a mile. Casualties had to be carried back, eight men struggling and slipping to deliver each litter. It was all the men could do to stay alive in such appalling conditions.

During the last third of May any fighting action was near impossible for men who were already exhausted. The troops simply tried to stay where they were - the front had bogged down.

Despite the weather, elements of the 6th Marine Division crossed the Asato River and entered Naha, the capital city of Okinawa, which had been reduced to rubble after the pounding it took from both naval and on-shore heavy artillery. A few Okinawan civilians who were hiding in the rubble of the city said they had seen only scattered five or six man Japanese patrols during the previous week.

Naha had no tactical value other than to afford the Americans a route south to the next objective. The city is located on a wide coastal flat at the mouth of the Kokuba River. The Kokuba Hills extend eastward from the edge of Naha along the north side of the Kokuba estuary and the Naha-Yonabara valley. They guarded the south-western approaches to the rear of Shuri - to which we were desperate to gain access.

The Japanese, upon evacuating Naha took positions in the high ground in the eastern part of the city and the semi-circle of hills beyond. There the fight on the enemy's left flank entered its next phase.

Since the crossing of the upper Asato River on May 23, the left (east) elements of the 6th Marine Division encountered

98

on-going opposition. Concentrated attacks continued for several days, resulting in many casualties while we gained ground hill by hill, through rain, mud and sludge as forces of the Army and Marines battled a determined enemy, pounding away in the quest for the most prized possession of Okinawa - Shuri.

The bright promise of enveloping Shuri faded as the fighting of May 23-26 brought the assault practically to a standstill. The Japanese had installed a large number of anti-tank guns and automatic weapons which swept all approach routes to the key hills. Mortars were concentrated on the reverse slopes. Had tanks been able to operate, our infantry could have, perhaps, destroyed the enemy's fire power and overrun the Japanese defenders, but the tanks were mired down in the mud. On May 26, three-and-a-half inches of rain fell.

For the veteran combat troops of the Japanese army, there was no rest once they were committed. With few exceptions they stayed in the line until killed or seriously wounded. Gradually, toward the end of May, more and more second-rate troops from reserve units and labor groups were fed into the Japanese line to bolster the thinning ranks of the combat infantry. Nothing illustrates the great difference between the fighting in the Pacific, and that in Europe as the small number of military prisoners taken on Okinawa. At the end of May, the III Amphibious Corps had captured only128 Japanese soldiers and the four divisions of the 24th Army Corps had taken only 90 prisoners. In the light of these prisoner figures there is no question as to the state of Japanese morale. The Japanese soldier fought until he was killed.

Casualties on the American side were the heaviest of the Pacific war. At the end of May, losses of American troops (Army and Marines) were 26,044 killed, wounded or missing. American losses were approximately one man killed for every ten Japanese who fell victims of the war. Non- battle casualties were numerous, a large percentage of them being psychiatric or 'combat fatigue' cases.

In one of my trips around the battleground area, I ran into a friend with whom I had served in the Beach Jumper Unit #1. He was attached to the 6th Marine Division as an infantryman. On two separate occasions he was the only survivor in his platoon. The first time was during an actual firefight. The second occurred when he and the rest of his platoon had taken shelter in a large crater made by shelling, probably from one of our ships. At dawn, the whole platoon was sitting around the rim of the crater having a smoke when a Japanese machine gun opened fire and killed every one of his comrades. He was not the same man I had known 18 months previously. He was an emotional and physical wreck. I felt terribly for him and embarrassed because of my cushy job compared to his.

American staff officers believed that the Japanese would fight at Shuri to the end. The struggle had gone on so long in front of Shuri that everyone, apparently, had formed the opinion that it would continue until the last of the Japanese defenders had been killed.

Actually, the Japanese had been preparing to evacuate Shuri, and in the waning days of May 1945, the movement of troops to areas toward the southernmost part of the island was under way.

As the battle lines tightened around Shuri, the 1st Marine Division and the Army's 77th Division stood closest to the town. Patrols reported no signs of weakness in the enemy's determination to hold the Shuri position. Invariably our troops drew heavy fire when they tried to move forward. After a protracted battle toward one of the most heavily guarded ground, the Marines led the charge, broke through all obstacles and took Shuri.

We in the G-1 Section had been scouting locations in this vicinity for the previous few days so were familiar with the area. On the day the 5th Marine Regiment of the 1st Marine Division secured this fortress, Colonel Cummings, Lt Coontz, Nick Breen and I were not far behind. We drove up to the town. Shuri, the second town of Okinawa, lay in utter ruins. There was no other city, town or village in the Ryukyus that had been destroyed so completely. As we

101

walked around the rubble, it was obvious that we were walking over the bodies of dead Japanese and Okinawans, buried in the debris. It was particularly disturbing to look down and see long black hair protruding from the jumbled remains of buildings - which meant that females had perished along with the soldiers and other citizens of Okinawa. This was one more very unpleasant experience.

Now that we had cracked Shuri, it appeared that the rest of the battle would be a matter of cleaning up pockets of resistance. However, there was none - the enemy had withdrawn all their forces from Shuri and had organized a new line of defense in the south. The enemy's surprise action, though it did not result in setting up a formidable line of defense, gave the American troops three crowded weeks of pursuit and fighting to bring their well-organized but weakened resistance to an end.

Mud was a major concern of American commanders. Nearly 12 inches of rain had fallen during the last ten days of May and more was expected during the first part of June. Although 400 trucks had been used on May 30 to dump coral and rubble into the mud-holes on the main north-south road through the center of Okinawa, it was closed the following day to all but the most essential traffic.

'We had awfully tough luck to get bad weather at the identical time that things broke,' General Buckner said.

Supply trucks were moving toward the front only as fast as they could be dragged by winches or bulldozers though the numerous quagmires.

The Japanese retreat, although harassed by artillery fire, was conducted with great skill at night and aided by the monsoon storms. The Japanese 32nd Army was able to move nearly 30,000 men into its last defense line on the Kiyan Peninsula, which ultimately led to the greatest slaughter on Okinawa in the latter stages of the battle, including the deaths of thousands of civilians. Some 4,000 Japanese sailors, including Admiral Minoru Ota, all committed suicide within the hand-built tunnels of the underground Naval headquarters on June 13. By June 17, the remnants of Ushijima's shattered 32nd Army were pushed into a small pocket in the far south of the island.

On June 18 the largest, slowest and bloodiest sea/land battle in American military history was dealt yet one more tragic blow. General Buckner had arrived at a forward observation post in his command Jeep, which was flying his standard three-star flag. Visits from the General were not always welcome as his presence frequently drew enemy fire, usually when he was departing. However on this day, he arrived with his three stars showing on his steel helmet. A nearby Marine outpost sent a signal to Buckner's position stating that they could clearly see the General's three stars on his helmet. Told of this, he replaced his own helmet with an unmarked one. However, a small flat Japanese artillery projectile of unknown caliber struck a coral rock outcrop next to the General and fragments went into his chest. He was carried by stretcher to a nearby aid station where he died on the operating table.

Ironically the last remnants of Japanese resistance fell just three days later, although some Japanese continued hiding, including the future governor of Okinawa Prefecture, Masahide Ota. General Ushijima killed himself by seppuku (a form of Japanese ritual suicide by disembowelment) in their command headquarters in the closing hours of the battle.

The battle of Okinawa would generate many 'firsts' for the history books beyond the first time that United States troops fought on Japanese soil. The battle occurred during a time of unprecedented historical significance. The two highest-ranking officers to die during the Second World War were the commanders on Okinawa, General Buckner and General Ushijima. Furthermore, General Roy S Geiger, a Marine, assumed command of the US 10th Army. It was the first time a Marine would command a fighting force as large as a field Army. He held that post for a short time before turning it over to General Joseph W Stillwell.

The command post of the III Amphibious Corps had moved from the north into the city of Naha in order to be closer to our troops. We undertook numerous tasks related to restoring order in the island colony. While assisting the Okinawans to recover and rebuild their lives, we had a responsibility to safeguard the welfare of our own troops. One duty thrust upon Colonel Cummings came unexpectedly but once more he proved himself capable.

As the campaign wound down, the citizens of Okinawa had come to realize that the Americans were not the demons the Japanese military had portrayed us as, but to the contrary were kind and generous. Consequently some of the young women on the island became attracted to our troops and offered themselves for sexual activity. This was not wide spread but co-habitation did occur. In most cases it went unnoticed but when a couple were caught in the act, mostly by the girl's parents, some cried: 'Rape' - and complaints were registered. Being a justice-seeking nation, some of our troops could have been convicted falsely, if it were not for the intervention of cool-thinking young military lawyers who were assigned to defend the men in courts martial. These young lawyers sought the advice of an officer who was not only knowledgeable but one who sought true justice. Colonel Cummings therefore accepted the responsibility of questioning the officers thoroughly to make certain that their clients were not guilty, then provided advice on how to bring out the truth, thereby vindicating the falsely accused military personnel. None was convicted and justice prevailed.

After 82 days the Battle for Okinawa, the most costly battle of the Pacific in terms of loss of lives, both military and civilian - and what turned out to be the final battle of World War II - was over. It was time to move on.

On July 3, 1945, I received orders dispatching me, along with 12 Officers and enlisted men, to report to the rear echelon of the III Amphibious Corps, USMC, on Guam, for duty. Okinawa had been secured and was completely under control of US forces.

We boarded the R4D, Transport plane, on the July 4 at Kadena Airfield and took off for the 1400-mile journey to Guam.

As we roared down the runway and lifted off, I reminisced about our landing on Okinawa and spent a couple of hours thinking about all the horrors of war and the loss of so many fine Americans.

My thoughts were interrupted by a change in the engine noise of the aircraft - one engine had quit.

While such a situation is not desirable, it was not a showstopper because those planes were rugged and we could manage with the other three. A short time later, however, we lost another engine. That had not reached the catastrophic stage because the second failure was on the opposite wing to the first. The pilot however, reckoned that we had better get on the ground as soon as possible and get all engines firing again. The problem of course, was that there was not any ground nearby. We were about halfway between Okinawa and Guam. We could either continue flying toward Guam, return to Okinawa or head for Iwo Jima which was a little further away.

The passengers, talking amongst themselves, elected to go to Iwo since none of us had ever been there and that would be an interesting adventure. Since the passengers held no sway in the voting, it was in the hands of the pilot. The weather report from Guam was not good and since we knew the weather on Okinawa was fair when we left, that was the choice made. We turned around and headed back northwest for the long haul back to Okinawa. As we approached the landing field, the third engine decided to quit also. It was a nail-biting time - but not for long. Although it appeared that we were coming in almost sideways to the runway; the pilot skillfully maneuvered the plane to a successful landing and headed to the repair area. The twelve passengers disembarked first, followed by the crew. To my surprise, the Navy Lieutenant who was the pilot looked as if he just barely met the height requirement for flight training. He reminded us that what was accomplished in the cockpit had nothing to do with height. We gave him three cheers.

Ironically, as we landed, the air-raid siren was sounded but no one was alarmed, as the Japanese had no punch left in the air. We hung around the airport and spent the night in the building serving as a terminal and the next morning, July 5, we took off again. This time we made it all the way to Guam with no further incident.

Back on Guam, we settled into our daily routine and wondered what was in store for us. The high-ranking officers were busy planning but we had no knowledge of what they were discussing. We could only guess and the future looked very bad. It was obvious that the next target would be the mainland of Japan but we knew not where. We were concerned though that it would be a bloody battle; unlike none we had been experiencing. On the two campaigns that I took part in, Guam and Okinawa, few civilians were involved. Anticipating a strike at the mainland, we knew that every citizen would be a combatant and every tool would be a weapon. It was not a comforting thought.

After distinguishing himself yet again on Okinawa, General Roy S Geiger was our Commanding General. Following General Buckner's death, the General had assumed command of the Tenth Army for a short time before being promoted to Commanding General of Fleet Marine Force, Pacific. Major General Keller E Rockey, formerly Commanding General of the V Amphibious Corps took command of the III Amphibious Corps and Brigadier General William A Worton took over as Chief of Staff.

We went about our duties until that night on September 2, 1945, when the whole game plan changed. It was in the evening and suddenly, the noise of voices shouting and chanting came closer and closer. The Japanese had surrendered to General Douglas MacArthur, Supreme Commander for the Allied Powers, on the Battleship USS Missouri in Tokyo Bay! Although we were aware that a small contingent of Japanese officials had arrived on the tiny island off the coast of Okinawa to explore the possibility of a surrender, there is no way to describe the pandemonium of the night except that it was filled with the sounds of jubilation. The realization that we would not have to fight and kill innocent civilians was an overwhelming relief, and that we would not have to come to terms with a staggering number of our own Sailors, Soldiers, Marines and Airmen who would not go home again.

Later I was to read General MacArthur's opening statement at the Japanese Surrender Ceremony and could only admire his generosity of spirit. In his speech were the words: 'It is my earnest hope, and indeed the hope of all mankind, that from this solemn occasion a better world shall emerge out of the blood and carnage of the past - a world founded upon faith and understanding, a world dedicated to the dignity of man and the fulfillment of his most cherished wish for freedom, tolerance, and justice'.

After what we had been through it was the heart-felt wish of every member of the Allied Forces.

CHAPTER TEN

CHINA ASSIGNMENT

Once the war was over speculation in our ranks rose to fever-pitch. Everyone wondered what was in store for us. We knew that those who had acquired sufficient seniority overseas would be heading home and those who did not make the cut would no doubt be engaged in occupation duty.

Seniority, or 'longevity' was expressed in terms of 'points' and I had not acquired sufficient to head home so I started dreaming up ideas. I approached Colonel Cummings about the possibility of being sent to Hawaii on temporary duty. My brother, having survived the battle for Guadalcanal, went back to the States but then was re-assigned to a unit in Hawaii to prepare to face the enemy again. I had missed my brother very much during the war years and wanted to be back in his company. Colonel Cummings approved my request and I prepared to take off on that boondoggle.

The evening before my scheduled departure I was summoned to Colonel Cummings's quarters. He started our conversation by re-affirming my travel to Hawaii if I so chose but had an alternative offer that he hoped I would consider favorably. He then told me that he, Eddie Coontz and Nick Breen, each had acquired sufficient points to return to the United States and would be leaving shortly. He went on to tell me that his temporary replacement was Colonel William D Crawford who would be acting G-1 and would be participating in a special mission led by our Chief of Staff, Brigadier General Worton.

The General had served several tours of duty in China before the war, knew the country well, knew many officials in high office and spoke more than one Chinese dialect.

The special mission he was assigned to was to enter North China immediately and establish relations with the commanding general of the Japanese Imperial Army headquartered in Tientsin and to commence arrangements for the eventual surrender of North China to the Allied Forces. As well he was required to liaise with both the Chinese Nationalist Party as well at the Chinese Communist Party. His team was to consist of five colonels, one navy captain, three captains, one first lieutenant and six enlisted men. I was Colonel Crawford's choice as one of the enlisted men. I had great respect for Colonel Crawford and General Worton and was overwhelmed by the opportunity so immediately accepted the offer. In addition to the advance party, there were four Chinese-born civilians who had volunteered to go with us as interpreters and another 16 enlisted men who were communication specialists.

While this was a whole new adventure for me, planning and preparation for the eventual liberation of North China had been on-going for some time. The selection of General Worton to take the lead in the initial entry into China must have been carefully calculated.

In 1935 - before World War II, but during the China/Japan conflict - the General had been assigned to a special operation in China. He was given a 'cover story' to pose as a disgruntled officer leaving the Marine Corps to establish a business in Shanghai. Under this guise he returned to China and began to recruit agents who agreed to travel to Japan to secretly collect information for the US Navy. Working with Chiang Kai-Shek's secret police he performed his assignment admirably and returned to Washington in June 1936.

As early as August 1945 the Commanding General, United States Forces, China Theater, issued a directive on the basic principles of civil affairs in China

Early in September 1945 the commanding general, III Amphibious Corps issued a 'concept of operation' for the upcoming occupation of North China. It spelled out the political situation in China and the military operations to be put in place prior to the Japanese surrender.

Our orders were to depart by air for China on or about September 18, 1945. We actually took off at midnight on September 17. General Rockey and several thousand Marines departed by ship on September 18 and would join us in Tientsin.

The advanced party flew in two R4D aircraft. General Worton had acquired an experienced pilot, Colonel Karl Day whom he knew during his service in World War I. Colonel Day left the military at the end of that war and had become a command pilot for American Airlines. When World War II broke out he re-entered the Marine Corps. The plane Colonel Day flew contained the members of our team. The second one was loaded with our supplies - a myriad of assorted goods. Not knowing where and if we could get gasoline, supplies were included in the cargo. Only General Worton, Colonel Brown, the G-2 and Lieutenant Walter Curley, the General's aide, knew another item that we carried. It was $3,000,000 in US gold coupons to be used for expenses and packed in boxes labeled "Thirty Caliber Rifles". These boxes were to cause us some concern when we arrived in Tientsin.

We flew first to Okinawa for refuelling. We arrived early on the morning of September 18. General Worton and Colonel Brown had breakfast with General Wood who commanded marine aviations on Okinawa. We got our fuel and headed out over the East China Sea - which had been a combat zone just a few days previously.

As we approached the airfield in Shanghai we circled and took a look at the field which was strewn with a considerable amount of shrapnel. The pilot decided it was safe to land, however, we picked up some of the debris and blew a tire on the way in. General Worton had instructed a few officers to remain with the aircraft and the rest of us were loaded into vehicles to be driven to our hotels on Nanking Road, just off the famous Bund. General Worton and Colonel Brown were quartered in the Cathay Hotel and the rest of us stayed at the Palace Hotel, across the street. This was quite a change from the tents we had been living in over the past few years. I actually experienced a bit of claustrophobia riding in cars, trucks and in elevators, which I thought was odd because I had never experienced that feeling in airplanes. However, the luxury of our surroundings soon banished those feelings.

Although our stay in Shanghai was brief it was an enchanting experience. Staying a stone's throw away from the Bund, the site of where this marvelous city was founded, sent thrills up and down my spine. This section of the city had undergone much reconstruction in 1930s under the influence of Europe, so it was a grand mixture of exquisite buildings with the teeming population of Chinese who were walking, cycling and riding in coolie-pulled rickshaws in droves.

While we were on temporary duty, we were essentially there as guests of the Japanese Army - who were still in control - and as such, any receipts we signed were paid by them. A couple of my pals and I got cute and went out looking for genuine booze for a party. There was a lot of locally manufactured stuff but in the liquor store in the basement of our hotel I came across several bottles of genuine whiskey which the proprietor had stored away. Since the Japanese were paying the cost was no object. I acquired half-a-dozen bottles of Scotch whiskey and several bottles of superior French wine. We then made reservations for a dinner party in the main restaurant of our hotel and went up and down Nanjing Road inviting about a dozen Chinese - who could speak some English - to join us. We had a royal good time and made a hit with our guests.

General Worton is one of my all-time heroes for his service to America and his service to the City of Los Angeles after he retired - but most of all because of the manner in which he stood by his people. My first meeting with him was memorable - and could have been disastrous had he been of a different disposition. While in Shanghai I received a phone call from Master Sergeant Battles who was in charge of the enlisted men in our group. He said that he was in General Worton's suite at the Cathay Hotel but had an appointment and needed someone to deputize for him as the General was meeting with naval officers from a US ship

116

that had just arrived and was tied up at the Bund. I went over and relieved the sergeant. With nothing to do, I sat down at the General's desk and made myself comfortable with a glass of his cognac and lit up one of his cigars. All of a sudden, the door burst open and in came the General. I was very embarrassed and was terrified that I was going to be reamed out for taking liberties. To the contrary General Worton just exclaimed: 'Son, I am going out with friends for dinner and need to find my hat'. He often used 'son' as a term of endearment with the younger generation. We scurried around and eventually located the hat. The General departed and nothing was ever said about the incident. I polished off the remaining cognac in my glass and waited until Sergeant Battles returned.

The next day we went back to the airport and took off for our final destination which was Tientsin. There were no maps to guide us so we relied upon General Worton's knowledge of the country. We flew northeast to Tsingtao and then cut across Shantung Peninsula and picked up the mouth of the Pei-ho River, which led us to Tientsin. Upon arriving Colonel Day took one look at the small field and said the runway was too short. General Worton shrugged and said: 'You have to get us in, those are my orders'.

Colonel Day responded: 'OK, I'll drag the field and take a closer look'. He communicated to the pilot of the other aircraft to standby and we made our approach. The next thing we knew we had landed safe and sound, stopping at the end of the runway just short of a rather wet marsh. The other plane came in safely as well.

A Japanese major met us and informed the general that General Omoto, the chief of staff of the North China Command suggested that we take up rooms at his headquarters but General Worton said that he was very familiar with Tientsin and wished to set up residence and establish our temporary headquarters at the Astor House Hotel.

At this time the true contents of the cases labelled 'Thirty Caliber Rifles' was known only to the General, Colonel Brown and Lieutenant Curley. As our stuff was being loaded on to Japanese trucks Lieutenant Curley whispered to General Worton: 'What are we going to do with the money?' General Worton told him to sit on the boxes on the back of the Japanese truck. He told him to make it appear that the cases were not important. With some degree of trepidation, but with his intense loyalty to the General, Lieutenant Curley followed orders and the task was accomplished.

When we got to the hotel, the General called a meeting and the rest of us were told about the contents of the cases – though the sum of money was unspecified. I believe it was one of the enlisted men who came up with the solution for reasonably safe storage. The general was to occupy two suites of rooms at the top of the stairway opposite the elevator on the second floor - which meant that he had two bathrooms. The boxes were stored in one of the bathrooms. The six enlisted men volunteered to stand guard duty around the clock outside the General's suites. We set up a desk and posed more as receptionists than guards. That turned out to be a wise move because we could screen anyone coming up in the elevator or on the stairs before they gained access to the General.

As we settled into our jobs, taking individual duties while maintaining a close liaison as a team, I began to understand the magnitude of the task that was before us and was amazed at the number of things that General Worton handled. The more I saw of him in operation, the more respect I had for him.

Shortly after we were established at the Astor House Hotel, General Uchida, Commanding General of the Japanese Forces and his Chief of Staff, General Omoto came to call on the general. They pledged their complete support and cooperation. General Uchida proclaimed that his troops were General Worton's troops and at his disposal even though the surrender had not yet taken place. General Worton concluded that an amicable relationship was required to maintain order because in addition to the presence of a large Japanese force, there were as many

Communist Chinese as there were Nationalists in the area. A balancing of all of these conflicting forces was necessary.

The day after our arrival, General Worton flew to Weihsien, a prisoner of war camp on the Shantung Peninsula, and arranged the immediate release of more than one hundred prisoners of a number of nationalities who we needed to maintain the economy of the area. Among them was Teddy Nathan, a British national who was the general manager of the Tangshan Mines and the general manager of the railroad. We provided them with much needed clothing and set up a kitchen at the Tientsin Club to feed them.

General Worton was a take-charge guy and although not assigned to do so, a couple of days later, he flew to Peiping, and established a headquarters there despite the fact that at this point, this was pretty much a '17-man operation' as the occupying forces were still on the high seas steaming toward us.

North China had been the base for Nazi operations and they were prominent in Peiping. The German Consul General, Andrew von Delwick came to see General Worton and extended his hand. When General Worton did not respond by shaking his hand - and ordered him to stand at attention - the Consul realized that he was a prisoner of war. The General informed him that he did not intend to throw him in prison because it would take too many men to guard him but warned that any false move would cause the US to intern him and all of his people. He advised him that 65,000 United States troops were on their way and we were prepared to deal with the Germans. He also told him to keep their women off the streets after 6pm. If any of our troops insulted any women before 6pm they would be punished but if the women were on the streets any later than that at night, they were looking for trouble. Having established his intention to claim Peiping, he returned to Tientsin to continue his mission.

While in Peiping, on this brief trip, General Worton was contacted and informed that a Senior Communist official wanted to call on him to discuss matters - to which he agreed. The meeting was set for 10pm. The visitor was Chou En-Lai, the second highest executive in the Communist Party. The meeting was very formal. Chou En-Lai was no stranger, as the General had known him during his previous tours of duty in China. The purpose of the call was to extend a welcome to our troops and to convey a special message. He said that he had heard that our troops were planning to occupy North China and acknowledged that, but said we would not be welcome in Peiping. If we intended to move there, he would do everything in his power to prevent us from going into that city. Having served in China for many years, the General realized that Peiping was to China as Washington, DC was to America or as Rome was to Italy. Whoever controlled Peiping controlled China. He also realized that if he had sought permission from Washington it would probably be denied so he took the bull by the horns. He told Chou En-Lai that he had already established a presence in Peiping and that the First Marine Division was going to enter Peiping and that they were one of the finest fighting units ever known and that it would be wise not to try to stop them. Chou En-Lai asked: 'Do you intend to occupy?' The General responded that he did intend to occupy and that was the end of the conversation and the visit. Hence, the First Marine Division under the command of Brigadier General Louis Jones occupied Peiping shortly thereafter without a shot being fired.

The General's concerns regarding women were based on reality. The troops who would be landing in North China had been slogging it out in the South Pacific islands for more than two years. Despite their reputation of being 'islands of love', they were hardly the locale for female companionship during the war. He envisioned some of the Chinese and European women in China could become available to our men and was very concerned that the men would contract sexually transmitted diseases (STDs). General Worton had been discussing this problem with our medical officer who said he had about 50,000 prophylactics (condoms) but they were four years old and probably past their use-by date, because there was so little use for them in the islands.

Lieutenant General Stratemeyer of the US Army Air Force had flown in from Karachi to coordinate our air operations with theirs and had a conversation with General Worton about his concern over providing protection against STDs. General Stratemeyer said that when he got back to Karachi, he would talk to his medical team to see if they could be of help. A few days later, a communications sergeant came rushing in with a radio message for the General from Karachi. The message read: 'I am shipping 1,000,000 condoms to you by air'. Within 10 minutes another message arrived from the Commander in Chief, Pacific Ocean Area, addressed to General Worton. The message was short - all it said was: 'What a man!' signed, simply, 'Nimitz' (Admiral Chester W Nimitz, United States Navy). That triggered a series of messages from the General's friends all over the world. A particularly notable one came all the way from the middle of the Mediterranean.

General Worton had a wealth of knowledge about the Orient. Many were concerned that we would run into difficulty with the Japanese but the General reasoned that Japan, having surrendered by order of their emperor to General MacArthur in Tokyo Bay, that the command we dealt with would be cooperative - and indeed they were.

123

One of his first actions after our troops landed in mass was to convene a board of officers to count the three million dollars - entrusted to him - and turn it over to the Corps paymaster. We all were greatly relieved to get rid of that responsibility. One can only speculate why that huge amount was allocated to our mission. Perhaps the powers that be in Washington felt that we might have had to flood the area with currency to maintain the economy in North China. However we maintained the economy by ensuring that all normal operations continued and that inflation did not become an issue. The Japanese had evidently realized that it was in the best interest of all concerned to allow businesses to flow without intervention so our mission was merely to allow market forces to continue to control the economy.

In response to queries from Headquarters about the condition in North China when we arrived, General Worton replied: 'The Japanese were deployed guarding the coal mines and maintained a perimeter of defense against the Communist troops as well as the Nationalists. North China was quiet when we arrived. Food was abundant, railroads were running and merchants were operating. There were no Communist forces in the cities of North China because the Japanese controlled the cities. There were however, large bodies of Communists within 75 miles of all of the cities'.

I found the Chinese people to be affable. They were

extremely pleased that we were there and greatly relieved that they were no longer under jurisdiction of the Japanese. There seemed to be little open resentment about how they were treated. I am sure there was some cruelty administered, but it was not apparent. Perhaps by allowing the Chinese to continue doing business as usual, there was no need to exercise brutality in this city. Having said this, when we began to repatriate the Japanese troops back to Japan, Chinese renegades would frequently attempt to seek revenge. On one occasion, we even had to re-arm a small number of Japanese troops to fend them off.

The Chinese who I met were friendly and courteous. Since I do not speak the language, many opportunities to communicate were missed, but everywhere I went, I was treated with care and kindness. Tientsin, even during my time there, was by no means a backward community. Housing for the most part was clean and well kept, despite the lack of modern facilities. It was commonplace to see carts in the streets with huge tanks of water for bathing. Many parts of the city were quite fashionable and well built. One of my favorite neighborhoods was the Italian quarter. The buildings are ornate and reminiscent of Italy itself. (It remains that way even today). The Pei-ho River, which is the gateway to the sea, was a busy waterway and, due to the amount of traffic, carried its share of flotsam and jetsam.

When we first arrived in September, the weather was warm with plenty of sunshine. Many of the Chinese, both men and women, dressed in traditional long gowns but there was a large segment of the population which sported western clothing. In the evening, those who dined out or attended theatrical and musical events were dressed in the finest garments. The men tended to wear suits complete with neckties and the women glamorous satin-patterned cheongsams in brilliant colors. The influence of the large number of Europeans who lived there may have been a factor in dress. There was a pleasant mixture of upscale shops that rivaled those in western countries. They blended in with the many outdoor markets featuring meats, vegetables and live chickens, even clothing and jewelry. Bargaining was normal wherever we went. Travel in the city was a mixture. Rickshaws and bicycles dominated the streets and roadways and the few automobiles were powered by 'gas producers' - a charcoal burning contraption either on the running board or in the trunk. When our gasoline-powered vehicles arrived they were a bit of a novelty. In the heart of the city all the streets were paved and well kept. The restaurants I went to could have been found almost anywhere in the world. Certainly there were the coffee shops and food stalls, but the up-market restaurants resembled those in New York City, Sydney, or even Paris. White linen tablecloths, silverware, glassware and menus were very western in style. The maitre'D and waiters all wore tuxedos, as they say, the whole nine yards.

As we were essentially functioning on behalf of the Chinese nation under the command of Generalissimo Chiang Kai-shek, whether or not he was involved, General Worton felt that it was necessary to make decisions without being bogged down by running everything through the high command.

In both Peiping and in Tientsin, it was necessary to take over various properties immediately. In Peiping these included the British legation, the German barracks and embassy and the American guard barracks. The same was true in Tientsin and we took over many properties, no matter to whom they belonged. There was no resistance except for one Vichy French colonel who denied us the right to take over their arsenal in Tientsin. He held that it belonged to France and he was going to keep it. General Worton confronted the colonel and said: 'If I send 2,000 of our troops against your 200, how are you going to keep it?' The colonel replied: 'Then we will fight you to the very last Frenchman'. General Worton responded: 'That would be silly', and smartly reported the conversation to General Wedemeyer, suggesting that the French Ambassador at Chungking get involved. We took over the arsenal.

I cite these vignettes to demonstrate the tenacity of a General who had the courage to act responsibly in every area on behalf of the United States government as well as the rest of the Allied Forces. He was awarded the Bronze Star (his second) and the Legion of Merit for his service in North China. I thought he deserved more for his actions as he carried out his assignment.

My guess is that President Truman, perhaps due to his service in the Army, was not fond of the Marines and therefore did not want to lavish too much opportunity or accolades on us. In comparison, General MacArthur had nothing but the highest praise for the Marines and was a supporter of our entering North China - while he was busy dealing with issues in Japan, Korea and Indo China. It is believed by many objective folk that if Washington was not in such a hurry to pull our troops out of North China we would have contained the Communists and prevented the Russians from penetrating into Manchuria and Korea and consequently there would not have been a war in Korea nor in Vietnam.

While General Worton was busy with all of the things he chose to devour, the rest of us were also carrying out a variety of activities related to our respective areas. For instance, Colonel Crawford and I represented the G-1 Section which dealt with personnel issues.

Colonel Crawford was a US Army officer - not a Marine. I have mentioned the brilliance of Colonel Gale T Cummings, who was the G-1 until just before the advance party left Guam. Colonel Crawford, whose expertise was finance, had previously been temporarily assigned to the US Marines III Amphibious Corps. Colonel Cummings recognized his abilities and reasoned that he could be an asset in our department. He organized to get him assigned as one of his deputies - an area totally outside finance. This assessment proved correct, and when the advance party was formed Colonel Crawford was assigned as the G-1, at least for that mission. A Marine Corps colonel would later relieve him.

Colonel Crawford determined that one area requiring immediate attention was housing for the thousands of American troops who were aboard ships and due to arrive within a few days. He chose to handle that task himself. Asians have totally different needs than we Caucasians, so there were a lot of restorations required in previously occupied Japanese barracks. He devoted much of his time to that task.

In addition to my stints at receptionist/guard duties, he put me in charge of all of the hotels in Tientsin. We figured that there would be plenty of people drifting into the city from all over and some control was required. What a strange assignment for a corporal! The hotels were advised to contact me whenever anyone required accommodation. I had some unusual requests but the most memorable was when the Mayor of Shanghai showed up in one of the hotels and was informed that I would have to approve his reservation. I was contacted and immediately went to the hotel. He was a gracious gentleman and when I assigned him to the premier suite in the hotel and he was very pleased. As soon as our duties as members of the advance party were over, I no longer had that authority.

Ironically, a few months later, the Mayor visited Tientsin again and was a fellow guest at a social function. He recognized me and affirmed how much he had appreciated my assistance.

Shortly after arriving in Tientsin I met Marianne and Eric Reil – mentioned in my Prologue and unknowingly a pivotal person in this whole memoir.

One evening I had been out with another Marine sampling the nightlife of the city. Somehow we got split up and he went back to the hotel alone. With perhaps a little too much booze in my system, I sat down on a bench outside an apartment building. Marianne and Eric were returning from dinner and spotted me. With an occasional armed Japanese soldier wandering around, no doubt imbibing the same type of beverage I had been consuming, they were concerned for my safety. They approached me and invited me to their apartment for a cup of coffee. As we chatted I sobered up and they drove me back to the hotel. They were an interesting and hospitable couple and we became friends. Eric was a journalist but he also knew his way around China. He had contacts and became a useful advisor on the purchase of building materials, which helped us out greatly.

Eric, Marianne and I would go out to dinner and, through them, I met other expats and sophisticated Chinese people with whom I socialized.

There was one chap I met who was from the Philippines. He played in a band so I saw him often and we became good friends. He invited me to his home where I met his charming but reserved Japanese wife. She dutifully served our meal but was too shy to dine with us. My friendship with him gave me access to other members of the band with whom I would often have a drink during breaks. Hungry for new musical material, they asked me for information on the latest American songs. I was not very helpful except for one suggestion. It was approaching Christmas so I gave them the words to one of Bing Crosby's hit tunes, 'White Christmas'. They prevailed on me to get up on the bandstand with them and sing it. The locals gave me a great reception but other Marines were not too impressed.

In the role of receptionist/guard, I had some unusual experiences. On one occasion when I was on duty a Russian woman came up the stairs and announced she wished to see the General. Before introducing her to him I searched for some background information and was advised that she was secretary to a Japanese general who owned a factory in Tientsin. She had become aware that a Russian man had been engaged to provide services to us and she merely wished to warn us that he had a shady background.

131

That information was to become very useful and, upon further checking, we did not employ him.

We had set up a room in one of the General's suites as a conference room. When the General was not immediately available we would ask the visitor to wait there and, for security, whoever was on guard duty kept them company.

Amongst the many frequent visitors there was a Japanese first lieutenant. He had graduated from a university in the United States with a degree in mining. An important mission of ours was to ensure that mining and the provision of coal to industries continued functioning so we needed all the expertise we could find. When General Worton heard about this Japanese officer, he recruited him and gave him considerable responsibility at a major mine. He became a valuable asset.

The lieutenant was fond of American cigarettes so he and I would light up from my pack while we chatted. Before I left him with the General, I would leave my opened packet for him to take with him when he left. He graciously accepted them. I concocted what I thought was a great idea. One day, as we sat talking, I told him that I was fond of the Colt .32 pistol, which Japanese officers carried, and suggested to him that I would trade a whole carton of American cigarettes for one of those pistols. This guy was cool. He took his pistol out and handed it to me to inspect.

I looked it over and handed it back to him. He then put it to my head and said: 'If I pull the trigger of this weapon you will be dead and I probably would not get away but I will have been vindicated'. With the gun firmly to my temple he waited for my response. I was at a loss as what to do. No point in trying to draw my .45-caliber pistol - it was too late for that. Apology did not seem to be the right thing either, so I mustered up all the courage I could and said to him: 'Either pull the trigger or get that damned gun away from my head'. Mister Cool paused for what seemed to be the longest time, then took the weapon down and said: 'You have insulted a Japanese officer - do not ever do that again'. He lowered the pistol and returned it to his holster. I told him that I was profoundly sorry for my inappropriate behavior and that I would never be that foolish again. I had learned a valuable lesson about respect. After that incident, we established a genuine friendship and the last time I saw him, I handed him a gift-wrapped package. It was a carton of cigarettes. I often wondered if he told that story to his friends.

I mentioned the mentality of the Japanese soldier who we engaged in the islands while the war was in full bloom and how surrender meant disgrace. In the case of the Japanese military personnel in North China, the whole scenario had changed. The entire empire of Japan had surrendered to the Allied Forces so these returning men did not bear a personal level of disgrace.

Getting around Tientsin was a fun experience and I soon located - and frequently visited - an excellent restaurant which was situated on the top floor of the jai-alai forum. Jai-alai, a 400-year-old game which originated in the Basque area of Spain, was one of two European gambling sports introduced into China – the other was horse racing – in the first half of the 20th century. The game came to Tientsin in 1934 and flourished for little more than a decade.

The maitre'D at the restaurant regularly suggested to me that I should attend the jai-alai games – in which I had absolutely no interest. One night, however, he told me he would not serve me dinner unless I promised to go to the games. Without much interest I agreed and, after dinner, encountered a most startling experience. As I entered the jai-alai arena an attendant greeted me and in excellent English asked for my name. He then led my friend and me to a private box. On the door was a brass plaque, which read: 'For the private use of Corporal William W Hook, US Marine Corps'. Wow! What was this all about, I wondered. We entered the box and ordered drinks. The waiter told us that the games were about to begin and suggested that we allow him to make a selection of bets for the nine games. So far, so good, I thought, so I gave him the amount of money he requested. As the games progressed he brought the tickets back and put them under the ashtray, advising us not take a look until all games were completed. At the end of the games, we retrieved them and discovered that lady luck (or something) was on my side. As they say: 'My Momma did not raise dumb children'. I concluded that the 'fix was on' and that my response should be appropriate. I had won the equivalent of about US $600, so I tipped the waiter $300, speculating that going 50/50 may be the right thing to do.

The next morning I received a phone call and the caller merely said that a Chinese gentleman wished me to share tea with him at a suite in a nearby hotel. Once more I obliged. When I arrived a man in servant attire welcomed me and led me to a room to await the appearance of the mystery man who came in shortly afterwards. As we sat and had our tea he told me that I had acted appropriately the previous night and that I clearly understood the rules of the game. He instructed me to attend the games four nights each week and to give the equivalent of $100 each night to the waiter to place bets. He further indicated that updated instructions would be given to me after the main body of our troops arrived in Tientsin. He also indicated that by the time I left China, I would be a wealthy man. Indeed, I managed to send a few thousand dollars to my savings account in the United States, when another event took place. It was not too long after our troops entered the city that General Rockey concluded that the games were rigged and ordered them to shut down. Darn, the bubble had burst.

Aside from that experience, I still had a good time doing my duty by day and managing some great nightlife as well. I met a lot of Europeans as well as Chinese and established some warm friendships. I even attended the iconic Tientsin concert hall for Chinese opera - which was my first exposure to this cultural gem. The assignment of the advance party lasted only for about three weeks but we accomplished a great deal in that short period and I was on my way to being a genuine 'China Marine'.

On October 1, 1945, a parade of the Marine Corps' finest of the Sixth Marine Division marched into Tientsin and came past the Astor House as I sat on my balcony observing the parade. Some of the marchers looked over in amazement and must have wondered: 'What the heck was this corporal doing in this splendid hotel?' I was full of pride because these guys had been slogging it out on the front lines during the past couple of years and were now relishing the joy of liberation, rather than another battle. The Sixth Marine Division has the distinction to have never been on American soil. It was formed on Guadalcanal in 1944 and disbanded in China in 1946.

On October 4 my temporary duty had been completed and I

returned to my normal routine as driver for the G-1. Colonel Harry E Dunkelberger relieved Colonel Crawford who returned to the Army. While welcoming Colonel Dunkelberger, I was sad to see Colonel Crawford leave. He had chosen me to accompany him and that was an honor - and working closely with him was a rewarding experience.

Colonel Dunkelberger had come from Washington and, as far as I knew, this was his only recent field assignment. He was a gentleman and perhaps in recognition of my duties during the past few years, was very gracious and allowed me a lot of leeway.

We had a station wagon. As an example of his generosity and compassion, he came up with a novel idea. Most of the time he dined at the Race Course Country Club, which had a classy restaurant and was not fairly close to his house. He almost always dined with Colonel Brown and suggested that Colonel Brown's driver and I could alternate driving them to dinner, which would free up the other car for our personal use.

An unofficial perquisite I enjoyed was access to alcoholic beverages. Unlike enlisted men, officers had the privilege of buying liquor from the PX. They received a list of the available brands each month and they would simply check off the products they wanted and pay cash for their purchases. Having several officer friends and the use of the car, I would pick up the rations for a few of them. I suggested to Colonel Dunkelberger that I could get his allotment also and deliver it to his house. He checked off only Scotch and Canadian Club. In the PX those two brands sold for 75 cents a bottle while the rest were a mere 50 cents. Without consulting him, I checked off a whole lot more, which I paid for so I always had a stock of all the booze my housemates and I could ever want. I had a pretty active social calendar and was a big hit with the folks with whom I dined and partied. Often they would not allow me to pay for meals since I provided the beverages. Life was good.

While General Worton had laid the groundwork, General Rockey moved swiftly in ordering everything necessary to receive the surrender of the Japanese, many of whom were in seclusion until this day of embarrassment. With humility, he chose a solemn ceremony so as not to prolong the agony of the Japanese.

The ceremony took place on October 6 in the street in front of our office and it went off like clockwork while thousands of Chinese civilians looked on. It was solemn and efficient.

The setting was particularly impressive. While the ceremony took place in the middle of the street, the background was a park, a charming and well-kept reserve that was bedecked with autumn flowers.

Our senior officers stood in a horizontal line slightly to the right of the front entrance to the building, a magnificent structure of blocks of stone. The guard of honor was positioned to their right. The senior Japanese officers were stationed to the left side of the entrance.

A table was positioned in the middle of the road, which contained the surrender document. General Rockey stood in the front, with General Worton directly behind him.

At the appropriate time, General Rockey stepped forward and sat at the table to sign the document of surrender. Following him, General Uchida took a seat and also signed the document on behalf of the empire of Japan.

We Marines hung out of windows and parapets of the building to witness the proceedings, which took no more than 30 minutes.

It should be noted that this ceremony focused on the surrender of Japanese forces 'In the Tientsin' area. Later another surrender of the 'Tsingtao' area took place where Japanese General Nagano surrendered the area to General Shepherd, Commanding General of the 6th Marine Division, USMC. Yet another surrender took place in Peiping where the Japanese in that area officially surrendered to General Keller E Rockey.

My friend, Jerry Labounty had arrived from Guam with the main force and it was great to be reunited with him. Jerry was a stenographer who provided great service to the top brass. As such, he had access to what was going on at the top of our organization and had the good sense not to share it even with his friends. His contributions afforded him a lot of influence and he was not at all shy in seeking special privileges. There was no demand for him as a stenographer in China so he switched to being a driver for Colonel Brown, the G-2 Officer. Since seven colonels had homes in a semi-private circle off Race Course Road, Jerry suggested that we acquire quarters for the seven drivers near-by so we could be available 24/7 if needed. Approval was granted and Jerry located a three-story, 23-room house practically within view of where the colonels stayed. It had been the residence of the French Ambassador. After two years of living in tents, such luxury was almost beyond belief. We each had a suite consisting of a bedroom, living room and bathroom. A few even had kitchens. We hired a couple of houseboys and a cook. Furniture was available for rent and inexpensive. Since we were living off-base we had allowances to purchase food. We knew our way around and managed to get some staples from the main base as well. Breakfast was about the only meal I participated in at the house as I almost always dined out in the evening. We even had a couple parties in the ballroom on the ground floor.

For seven enlisted men with the rank of corporal, (our rank was limited to our duties), we were living high on the hog.

When reminiscing about my China years I think of the many opportunities that I missed. I could have bought and shipped home Chinese treasures such as antiques, silk and jewelry - which were all very cheap - with my earnings from jai-alai.

There were also business opportunities, on which I could have capitalized. I met several businessmen who wished to form partnerships with me. One day a Chinese gentleman invited me to lunch and suggested that I bring six of my friends. He indicated it would take up most of the afternoon. When we arrived at the nominated restaurant we were seated in a private room with a huge round table. Next to each guest was a young lady whose duty was to serve Chinese delicacies to each of us and to keep our wine glasses topped up. The meal was a delicious Chinese banquet of many courses and lasted about three hours. Afterwards, our host suggested that he and I have a private meeting. My impression was that I had been under observation and he satisfied himself that his judgment of me had been correct. My close association with officers during the previous few years caused me to feel as though I had had some tertiary education, even though I had not even graduated from high school.

The Chinese gentleman was wealthy and, now that the war was over, was interested in an import/export venture. He proposed that after I had returned home and was discharged I should be his business partner, receiving products from China to market in the US. He wanted me to arrange for items - which he would identify - to be shipped from the US to China. Realizing that I was not likely to have sufficient funds to run my part of the arrangement, he offered to bear all costs of setting up the business. I turned him down and that may have been when I forfeited my first opportunity to become a millionaire.

As a young Marine I was more interested in the present than in the future - I had not yet turned 21 and my focus was certainly not on the rest of my life. Even after our supporting troops had arrived, I continued to visit excellent restaurants and spend many nights at the theater. My favorite restaurant remained the one on top of the jai-alai forum, even after the games were shut down.

One problem I had was the midnight curfew for enlisted men, which rather cramped my style. I thought I should deal with it. After the surrender, there were many military personnel of all ranks visiting Tientsin. As a port city, we had many US Naval vessels coming in and the officers soon started appearing at the restaurants I patronized. I worked out a solution to my problem: as midnight approached, I would go to a table where high-ranking officers were dining and spin a story to the highest ranking officer. Navy captains were my favorites. I told them that I was soon departing and that my friends were having a farewell party for me. I explained my problem with the curfew and asked if, when the MPs did their rounds advising enlisted personnel to depart, they could do me a favor by saying I was their driver for the evening. Most of the officers I solicited were only too happy to oblige. Generally the MPs took my word for why I was staying on at the restaurant and the few times they questioned me closely, my co-conspirator backed me up.

Driving home after one of these occasions, at about 2am, I clipped a rickshaw. I stopped to make sure the driver was not injured and to work out an arrangement to get the rickshaw repaired. Things were going fine until the military police showed up. They concluded that I was in violation of the curfew, no doubt intoxicated and had unauthorized passengers in a military vehicle. No longer under the cover of my Navy officer advocate, I was not in a position to avoid getting a summons.

The next morning, I alerted a pal in the office of the adjutant to be on the lookout, and learned that indeed, the warrant had been delivered to his office. Swift action was required and I determined that I might have one ally who had the clout to bail me out. I went to the office of General Worton and told him the story. He sprang into action and phoned the adjutant, a captain who had served under the General on previous tours of duty. He asked if he had the summons issued to Corporal Hook. The adjutant responded: 'Do I ever', whereupon the General said: 'I want you to tear it up and put it in the trash. It never happened'.

The captain then told General Worton that he had already notified the HQ & Services Battalion and was ordered to send the summons to a certain lieutenant colonel. This was none other than Scrooge - the fellow I had so angered by taking him behind enemy lines on Guam. After his voting assignment in the general election he was ordered to remain in the field in a prominent position in the Headquarters and Service Battalion instead of returning to Washington. He never forgave me for 'putting him in danger' and was determined to 'get even'. This appeared to be his opportunity. General Worton was aware of the Guam incident and was determined that vengeance was not appropriate, so he told the captain to advise the colonel that he had not actually seen the summons but had heard about it and that in fact it was not Corporal Hook but was someone entirely different and not even in our jurisdiction. He said: 'Captain, do you understand what I have said?' Apparently he did and his allegiance to the General prevailed. Then General Worton told me that he felt that the malaria I had picked up on Guadalcanal had evidently flared up and I was to report to sick bay for a few days to allow this whole thing

144

to blow over. While in bed 'recuperating' I received a visit from Scrooge who had some choice expletives and a threat that one day, he would 'get me'. I of course denied any knowledge of what he was talking about.

Our operation began winding down and I had acquired sufficient points to go home. The same was true with my friend Jerry Labounty. Jerry and I concocted a scheme. We persuaded Colonels Brown and Dunkelberger to authorize air travel for us. In those days military travel was the only option - there was no such thing as a ticket from Tientsin to San Diego - rather it was a case of catching a flight from one city to another, where arrangements were negotiated to put in place the next leg. That suited Jerry and me just fine. We planned to fly from Tientsin to Shanghai, then to Tokyo, on to Manila, Hawaii and San Diego to report into Camp Pendleton and eventually to the east coast for discharge. We had envisioned staying in each place until we were satisfied, then moving on to the next port by offering souvenirs to pilots to get on flights. We estimated that it might take six months to get home. Naturally we did not tell Colonels Brown and Dunkelberger of the leisurely trip we had planned - but they were not born yesterday either and decided that we should travel by ship where only one carrier was involved. Headquarters and Service Battalion cut the orders - mine were to embark on one day and Jerry was to join the ship the following day.

145

As it turned out, it appeared that my pal, Scrooge, was aware of our comradeship and once more attempted to put a spoke in our combined wheels. The ship on which I was a passenger sailed that day. What he did not realize however, was that the ship would make another port call in Tsingtao, further south. Jerry immediately reported the situation to Colonel Brown who arranged to send Jerry by air to Tsingtao to await the arrival of the ship, so he had three days of fun there before joining me for the journey home.

The ship was the USS Wakefield - manned by the Coast Guard. It arrived in San Diego on February 1, 1946. Any mention of the Coast Guard manning a sea-going transport may be surprising to many who believed that the Coast Guard served only around the vast coastline of the US but that is not true.

Before leaving China though, I must make a confession related to the methodical way the military works. When we first arrived in China, traffic travelled on the left side of the road - as it does today in Japan. For some reason, as occupiers, we needed to do something about that so a decision was made to switch from driving on the left side, to the right side. I have no idea where this was dreamed up, but the American commanders decided to do it anyway. That makes perfect sense to Americans and mainland Europeans but British-influenced countries (and the Japanese former occupiers) may disagree. If this switch of driving habits seems strange, consider when we chose to put the new driving regime into effect. Of course it was the most logical time of the year - midnight, December 31, 1945. Fortunately, there were not too many automobiles on the road in those days but the new rule surely created havoc with the rickshaws, trishaws and bicycles.

Getting back to the Coast Guard, recently I was talking to my friend, Mike di Monda, a former Coast Guard veteran who served up and down our coasts as well as in Cuba, Saudi Arabia, Vietnam and all over Europe. He shared this story:

'A little known piece of history is that a 23-year-old member of the Coast Guard was the only member of that service to receive the Congressional Medal of Honor. Douglas Albert Munro received the award posthumously for his actions as officer-in-charge of a group of landing craft on September 27, 1942 during the September Matanikau action in the Guadalcanal campaign of World War II.

'The Medal of Honor citation reads:"For extraordinary heroism and conspicuous gallantry in action above and beyond the call of duty as officer-in-charge of a group of Higgins boats, engaged in the evacuation of a battalion of Marines trapped by enemy Japanese forces at Point Cruz, Guadalcanal, on September 27, 1942. After making preliminary plans for the evacuation of nearly 500

beleaguered Marines, Munro, under constant risk of his life, daringly led five of his small craft toward the shore. As he closed the beach, he signaled the others to land, and then in order to draw the enemy's fire and protect the heavily loaded boats, he valiantly placed his craft with its two small guns as a shield between the beachhead and the Japanese. When the perilous task of evacuation was nearly completed, Munro was killed by enemy fire, but his crew, two of whom were wounded, carried on until the last boat had loaded and cleared the beach. By his outstanding leadership, expert planning and dauntless devotion to duty, he and his courageous comrades undoubtedly saved the lives of many who otherwise would have perished. He gallantly gave up his life in defense of this country".'

We Marines who served in the Pacific knew the Coast Guard 'had our backs' and were grateful for their support and service to the Marine Corps and our country.

Jerry and I reported in to Camp Pendleton for a few days while they arranged to get us back to where we would be discharged. A not-so-funny event took place in San Diego. We were allowed liberty and were looking forward to 'doing the town'. On the first night back on American soil, the Marine Corps granted a $50 partial payment of our wages to roughly half of the troops – chosen alphabetically. I received my money - Jerry had to wait until the next day - but we took off together for fun and games. We encountered a wonderful bar and grill where we had dinner and drinks, got to know a happy band of locals and managed to blow most of my $50. The next day, Jerry received his $50 so we headed back into the city to the same bar. This time however, we met the resistance of the Women's Christian Temperance Union (WCTU) who demanded to see proof of age. Jerry had passed the age of 21 so he was okay but I was four months shy so I told the nice women that we had not been issued any ID yet, hoping to escape their interference. They did not buy that tale. The owner of the bar even came out and told them that we were there the previous night and were well behaved but that did not cut any ice so we were denied admittance. We attempted a couple of other bars but the ladies had the whole city under control. We ended up going to a movie.

We were in Pendleton for three days before being sent home for discharge. Jerry lived in Indiana, so he was sent to The Great Lakes Naval Station. My home was in New York so I was sent to the Navy Training Center in Bainbridge, Maryland where I was discharged from active duty but did remain in the Inactive Reserves.

It was my intention to write about my experience in China but not to get into the events that took place after I left in January 1946, however, I was intrigued by a story a new-found friend at a China Marine Association reunion told me. He had written it to preserve a memory of what could

149

well have been his last days, not only in China, but also on earth. Here is the story in his words:

'My name is John Ahigian and this is about 12 lucky Marines and a brave Chinese train engineer to whom we probably owe our lives. It was May 1947 and I was one of the last 30 Marines who stayed behind in Peiping (now Beijing) as our forces were being withdrawn from the most northern areas of China. Most of the Marines and all of the American civilians had left. There were 30 Marines left at the American legation remaining to take care of final matters. The Chinese civilians were sad to see us departing, as they felt protected while we were there. Transportation was mainly by train and trucks. There had been fighter planes at both of Peiping's airports but they were gone now. Travel was dangerous because the Chinese Communists were all around us. Americans were supposed to be neutral but we were linked to the Nationalists.

'The last few days in Peiping were memorable. "Hey Ahigian, wake up, it's 11:30, get ready for guard duty". That would be the last sleep I would have over a stretch of 42 hours. I jumped off my cot, got dressed, put on my heavy helmet, adjusted my ammunition belt and grabbed my M1 rifle. My post was at the front gate and the shift was midnight to 4am, the worst of hours for guard duty.

'Eighteen of our guys had already left for Tientsin a week

150

previously, so there were only 12 of us left in Peiping. This early morning, the weather was mild. There were only a few people in the streets, mostly on bicycles. No cars, trucks, or buses. It was a spooky feeling. We too would be leaving in approximately an hour after I completed my guard duty. There had been a brief ceremony the week before. The flag was lowered for the last time in Peiping and no Americans would be there again for 25 years. The Chinese civil war would be lost to the communists. My guard duty would be the last one by an American in Peiping.

'During this last watch, I was wide-awake and alert. There was only one other Marine sentry at the rear gate of the compound. The city of Peiping was quite safe but it was dangerous in the countryside. We understood that there were about 25,000 communist troops in that area. We would soon be exposed to them, as our path on the train to Tientsin would be threatened by their presence.

'On watch from midnight until 4am, time goes by slowly and thoughts of former times come back. The weather now was ideal but I could not help but remember a horrible time the previous December when I was on the same watch at the Italian Legation. I was assigned to the 1ˢᵗ Engineer Battalion of the 1ˢᵗ Marine Division. My post was from the front gate to the rear of the dark, isolated compound. Snow had already started the previous afternoon and it was now

blizzard conditions. I walked the post in knee-deep snow, the wind howling, with perhaps five feet visibility. There were no outdoor lights and by the time I reversed my direction, the billowing snow had covered my foot tracks. The heaviest clothing I had was a field jacket, which was fine for spring but hardly adequate in the cold winter snow. We had not been issued parkas and I was soaked through during the entire watch.

'I prayed for my replacement to be on time at 4am, and when he arrived, I ran as fast as I could through the deep snow to my barracks. After getting out of my wet clothes, I jumped into my bunk and hunkered down under my two blankets to try to thaw out. In just about an hour, I was up again for roll call. As I stood in formation and my name was called, I could not respond because I had lost my voice. I waved my arms franticly as the top sergeant called my name, "Ahigian".

'Two weeks passed and I could not even speak in a whisper. The top sergeant said I had to report to the hospital. The next day, another Marine drove me to a hospital at the other end of the city. I don't know who ran this small hospital. The nurses were foreign nuns. All the other patients were also Marines. I saw a Navy doctor when I checked in and then only one other time while I was there for two weeks. They ordered me to stay in bed. Every so often, they brought me a bowl of hot water, which I was

supposed to inhale with a towel covering my head. That
was the extent of my treatment.

'I was alone in the room and saw a nurse a couple of times
during the day. They popped in with my hot water and my
meals. It was a lonely time for an 18-year-old Marine, on
the other side of the world with Christmas approaching.
This was to be my first of two Christmas's overseas. Under
the doctor's orders I was to remain in bed. After three days
I decided to take matters into my own hands and do it 'my
way'. I got out of bed, ate meals in the mess kitchen and
visited the small lounge where other Marines gathered.
This room had a Christmas tree with other decorations. No
one there knew that I was supposed to be a bed patient.
Hospital life improved by just being out of my lonely room.
It was good to make contact with people even though I
could not talk. There was another Marine from my
company in the hospital. He laughed and thought it was
funny that I could not talk. It was nice to see him in good
humor because both of his arms were in casts.

'Christmas came and went and on the tenth day, I saw the
Navy doctor for the second time. He was surprised that I
was still unable to speak. After about four weeks of silence,
my voice slowly came back. I thought I might never talk
again. The diagnosis was acute laryngitis.

'Finally after another two weeks, I was discharged. No one

153

had contacted me from my Battalion during this period, so I was on my own. I went outside and was confronted by 20 rickshaw boys all at once. I was seeking only a bicycle-driven rickshaw since it was quite a distance to my barracks. I struck a bargain eventually and was on my way back to the Italian legation. It felt good to be able to talk again.

'Back from my reverie, time dragged on this last watch. As I patrolled my station at the main gate, I hoped the guy at the rear gate was equally alert, as I did not want to be the only one guarding this whole place. I have always taken my duties seriously and strove to be a model Marine.

'At this point in time, the civil war in China was at its peak. Our Marine forces were depleted and at its lowest level since we came here in September of 1945 so we were spread thinly. Our orders were not to engage the Communist Army and only protect ourselves. We were supposed to stay neutral. About six weeks previously, one of our Marine units at the Hsin Ho Ammunition Dump near Tangku had been attacked and we lost five Marines who were killed and 16 more wounded. We were always conscious of the possibility that we too might come under fire.

'The attack at Hsin Ho changed my next tour of duty. I had received orders in March that upon leaving China, I would

154

report to Camp Pendleton, California reporting to the First Marine Division.

'The Fifth Marine Regiment needed replacements for those killed at Hsin Ho. I had been looking forward to stateside duty and California was looking great in my sights. Instead, I was now to report to the Fifth Marine Regiment of the First Marine Division, which was now forming on Guam. The Fifth Marine Regiment was the most decorated unit in the Marine Corps. When I joined the infantry unit on Guam, we went on to become the number one combat-ready regiment in all of the Marine Corps. Our Commanding General, Edward Craig made us new replacements aware of this. I still have great pride in having served in this famous unit.

'It was 4am and my final guard duty in Peiping was over. We would be leaving in about one hour. I rushed back to our barracks and packed the last few items. No coffee now. For the past few days it has been 'C' or 'K' rations. The water was not suitable to drink so there was not much chow for the past week.

'We loaded our sea bags in the trucks for the short ride to the train yard. When we arrived, Chinese Government officials were there to take our trucks. An enormous amount of equipment was left behind. A system was in place as to how things were turned over to them. I

155

recognized the train station as I had driven there for my commanding officer a few times before when I was in the Engineer Battalion.

'The train was of early 1900s vintage pulling old boxcars. Our destination was Tientsin, which was about 90 miles southeast. The top-ranking Marine in charge of our small group was a sergeant. He gave us our orders before we boarded. There would be no more than one man in a boxcar. We were to leave the sliding doors open on both sides for good visibility. We were issued 200 rounds of ammunition (25 clips) for each man. Our orders were to put a clip in the rifle and a bullet in the chamber, safety on, and fixed bayonets. I don't like loaded guns but I concluded that we were not going on a picnic and we might have to fight in desperation. I boarded my assigned boxcar and about 6am, the engineer eased out of the station and we were on our way.

'We were soon beyond the walls of Peiping and into the desolate countryside. I recall that it was a bright sunny day, clear and we could see long distances.

'It was not too long before the train came to a full stop. The train engineer was talking to some village people. The sergeant got off and headed to the front of the train to talk to the engineer. None of us knew what was going on and we could not really hang too far out of the boxcars to talk to

156

*each other. We could have used some 'scuttlebutt' (gossip)
but came up empty. The train jerked, then started going
backwards, very slowly and a bit later the train stopped
again, before starting again on to another track direction.
The same thing happened again shortly thereafter, and at
least one more time. In the middle of the afternoon, another
Marine joined me in my car. I think the sergeant reasoned
that if we were ambushed, we would be safer with more
concentrated firepower. For the first time that day, I was
able to talk to someone. We surmised what was happening.
One of the stops was made because at one point the tracks
had been blown up. Once again, when the train stopped,
the Chinese civilians warned the train engineer about the
whereabouts of Communist troops in the area. We could
have been trapped but the help the train engineer received
from the villagers coupled with his knowledge of the
topography and optional track routes probably saved our
lives. When he backed the train up for miles at a time, he
was careful not to cause the train to jump off the tracks. He
was not only a skilled engineer but was also faithful to the
Marines whose lives were literally in his hands.*

*'Surviving Boot Camp at Parris Island was one of life's
toughest challenges, but it prepared me mentally and
physically for what we were going through right now. None
of us was actually worried or afraid but we kept on our
toes. I think each one of us was resigned to the fact that we*

157

were in dangerous territory and were mentally prepared to fight to our last breath if necessary in the tradition of all of the China Marines who preceded us. Surrender would not have been an option. I think the twelve of us could have outfought 500 of those who might challenge us. After years have passed since then, I realize how lucky we were to get through that experience unscathed, and thought that most of my family would not be in this world today. I guess that is called, "fate".

'At 6pm we arrived in the Tientsin railway station and were grateful for our skilled and dedicated train engineer who brought us through the 12-hour ordeal of travel forward and backward with several changes in direction. This was the same station I had left from the previous fall to join the Engineer Battalion in Peiping. We unloaded our sea bags and were pleased that we did not have to unload other supplies.

'No one was there to meet us, probably because we were so late in arriving. About two hours later, trucks arrived to transport us to our barracks. After a long day, 12 hungry, thirsty, tired and dirty Marines were looking forward to food, water, a shower and some rest. We got our shower and beds but the cooks would not open the mess hall because it was closed for the night. I could add that to my long list of reasons why not to re-enlist and sent a warning letter to my friend Pibby back in the States who was getting

overly "gung-ho".

'The next morning we were up early and had a huge breakfast in the mess hall, after which we boarded another train which would take us from Tientsin to Tangku, which was not far from where we lost Marines the previous month when the Chinese Communists raided the Hsin Ho Ammo Dump. After five days, we left for the port town of Taku where we boarded the USS Renville and sailed the next day for Guam, where I joined the 1st Battalion of the 5th Marine Regiment. I was there until early 1948 when I finally returned to the United States.

'A total of 53,000 Marines served in North China after World War II. In spite of hardships and loneliness, China was an unforgettable experience for my Marine brothers and all other military.

'Reports showed that the Chinese Communist Army had grown to 25,000 in May 1947 along the Peiping-Tientsin corridor. They were within 20 miles of the Peiping walls. How then did we miss contact with them? The train engineer knew all of the optional track routes and received valuable information from the villagers along the way. The Communists were misinformed that all the Marine forces had left weeks prior to our departure. This may be speculation on my part and we may not have been cognizant of the danger we might have been in. The twelve Marines

159

who survived this ordeal may not be much of a story compared to what happened in the Pacific Islands but we rejoice that in the end, we got the last of the supplies delivered.'

Thanks to John for sharing this missing piece of history. John and I have spent a lot of time together at reunions and at his summer home on Cape Cod.

If there is any doubt about who the main character in this writing is, let me make my intention crystal clear. Brigadier General Worton won my admiration from the very first time I met him until his passing in 1973.

He retired from the Marine Corps in June 1949 as a Major General and returned to his home with his wife in Carlsbad, California.

Immediately upon his retirement, he was requested by the mayor of the city of Los Angeles to discuss a special mission. The chief of police had been indicted as well as the assistant chief. The morale of the police department was shattered and crime was rampant. According to the charter of limitations one could not be appointed chief of police without having served actively in the Los Angeles Police Department. However the mayor could make an appointment of a temporary chief in an emergency for a period of 120 days. After an eight-hour session, the mayor prevailed on General Worton's sense of civic duty to accept the job. He was re-appointed four times and served for a total of 14 months. During that period, he gained the respect of the officers, the mayor and the public by taking daring moves to restore order within the department, while putting a lot of the bad guys in jail. One only needs to read the numerous accolades written in the newspapers over his achievements over that short period of time to realize the contribution he made to that city. This was one more victory for a fine officer.

CHAPTER ELEVEN

GOING HOME – MAKING A FAMILY

Before I went overseas as a young Marine I had become engaged to Rosalie Hale who lived in Wilmington, North Carolina, 52 miles south of Camp Lejeune where I was stationed before shipping out. While I was overseas, I cemented the pledge by purchasing an engagement ring, which I bought in the PX (of all places). Some years later I stole that ring - which Rosalie had taken off while washing dishes - and, after working with a local jeweler, surprised her with a more elegant ring on an anniversary of our marriage.

I returned to the US in February 1946 and was discharged in March. Immediately I headed back to Wilmington and Rosalie and I were married in April.

On April 10, 1948 we were blessed with the arrival of identical twins, Jean and Joan. (The bills from both the hospital and the doctor were paid with my winnings in a crap game at the Elks Club, where I worked as a bartender.) Not only are Jean and Joan identical but are what is known as 'mirror twins' - Joan is right-handed and Jean is a lefty. As my earnings were skimpy, luxuries were not in abundance around our apartment in the Lake Forest Community but we did manage to buy a washer with a wringer attached to launder the many diapers and other garments that, at times, seemed to overwhelm us.

On September 13, 1949 God showered another blessing on us with the birth of Sharon. Three toddlers in diapers kept that washing machine very busy. As they grew older the antics of our three little girls running around was quite a challenge, although delightful.

I could cite endlessly the many reasons for cherishing our three girls but one incident stands out above all the rest. While they were very young, we went to Fort Bragg, North Carolina for a weekend visit with one of Rosalie's sisters whose husband was an officer in the US Army. Our girls went out to play with their two cousins who were about the same age. After a time, their cousins returned but Jean, Joan and Sharon were not with them. A bit later they came back and asked us why their cousins did not want to play with their new-found friend, the daughter of another officer. We could not answer the question until we met the little girl. She was black and our daughters were obviously color blind. That incident warmed our hearts and made us feel that we were probably pretty good parents.

An allied situation made me equally proud of my church. In Wilmington, North Carolina, the Roman Catholic Church we attended was on 5th Street. Mostly Caucasians populated it. There was another Catholic church about three blocks away which was attended mainly by black people. Whether it was by design or whatever, I do not know, but the masses at our church began on the hour while masses at the other church began on the half hour. When we arrived late at our church, we simply went to the other one, and the folks who regularly attended the other church followed the same practice. Consequently, when the diocese office announced the end of segregation in churches in the early 1950s, our comment was simply: 'so what else is new?'

Things were tough for us in those days. Without a high school diploma it was hard to get a good job. I could not even get hired as a clerk in the Sears Roebuck store, even though I felt that my association with officers during my Marine Corps days had furnished me with a semi-college education.

After tending bar at the Elks Club, I worked with the husband of one of Rosalie's older sisters. Oscar Darrel had a wealth of knowledge about farming and we would drive to farming communities in North and South Carolina and fill his truck with fresh vegetables. We would buy such things as beans, watermelons or tomatoes, and then scramble to a farmers' market in the early hours of the morning to sell to wholesalers or store owners. Our objective was to be the first with the freshest crops. Sometimes we struck it big, other times, we found the markets flooded and were lucky to make expenses. Although Oscar Darrel treated my kindly, I was working very hard and not getting any richer.

I was determined to move up the ladder, so I managed to get a part time job at the J C Penney store on Front Street and enrolled in night school for a time, mostly learning skills such as typing. After eight months I took the high school equivalency test and received what amounted to a diploma. On a roll, I entered Wilmington College. After completing only one year, in September 1950, I was recalled in the Marine Corps since the Korean conflict had broken out and I was in the Reserves. We were the first to be activated. Goodbye to college. Fortunately, I reported in to Camp Lejeune, which allowed me to get home pretty often, but on a corporal's pay, we struggled. With eight years of longevity, I had considered making the Marine Corps a career, but that was not a popular topic of conversation around the Hook household. Rosalie was quite disenchanted about the prospect of me being shipped out to Korea, leaving her with three toddlers.

Fate entered the picture when the Marine Corps offered me an honorable discharge because of my rank and limited income. An Elks Club friend, Bill McKee, who owned an ice and coal supply company in Wilmington, offered me a

165

job managing his small business. I felt that I had no choice, so I took the discharge 89 days after being recalled.

Bill, who was a good friend as well as my boss, did an amazing thing about a year after he rescued me. He came in one morning at 7am and told me that I had earned more money for him in that year than he had ever made before. Then he fired me. Years later, he confessed that he had a motive for doing so. He reasoned that if he released me I could find a better job - which I did. At the time, however, it was a big shock.

I had joined the Elks Club as a member. Not everyone is familiar with the Elks so here is a synopsis of what it is all about. The Benevolent and Protective Order of Elks (BPOE) was originally formed in New York City as a social club but evolved into a fraternal, charitable, service organization with the emphasis on 'charity'. It supports national and local programs; which contribute to charity and service to military veterans and youth programs. Each Lodge has an Exalted Ruler, and three other chair offices: The Esteemed Leading Knight represents charity, The Esteemed Loyal Knight represents justice The Esteemed Lecturing Knight represents Brotherly Love. There are other offices as well; the most prominent of the lesser offices is that of Esquire. During my years in Wilmington as an Elk, I had the privilege of serving as Esquire and each of three chair offices. I probably would have risen to the position of Exalted Ruler had I not moved away from Wilmington. Perhaps my greatest contribution to the Elks was the deliverer of the Eleven o'clock Toast, which is a solemn tribute to those Elks who have passed on.

Through my affiliation with the Elks, I was associated with key people in Wilmington, a city of some 45,000 people, including one chap who was engaged in his family wholesale lumber business. He had told me that if I ever left Bill McKee's Ice and Coal company, that I should see him to discuss a business proposition. Consequently, the morning I got sacked, I went to see John Colucci to see what he had in mind. In those days, plywood was just beginning to rise in popularity. Until this period, it had been used primarily for cabinetwork. As such it was stocked in short supply by lumberyards. John predicted an exponential growth in its applications - for flooring, sheathing, roofing and many other uses. His offer was straightforward. He admired my work ethic and thought we could put together a company. He proposed a 50/50 partnership. The plan was to purchase a pick-up truck. I would use the truck to call on lumberyards and contractors to acquire orders for plywood at lower rates than they were paying. We would buy a freight car load, park it at his family's railroad siding and I would deliver the orders to customers. He envisioned that we could move a carload once each week, the period allowed by the railroad without having to pay demurrage. He was willing to put up the capital if I would do the work.

Rosalie and I talked over the proposition and together concluded that this would not be in our best interests as a family, for a number of reasons, so I turned the proposition down. As John had the plan well thought-out, he went ahead anyway. One year later he was importing shiploads of plywood and his office complex was an entire pier on the Cape Fear River along which the ships came up from the sea. That was the second time I had forfeited the opportunity to become a millionaire.

Instead, I went to work as a clerk in the freight department of the Atlantic Coast Line (ACL) Railroad. I worked in a room with about 90 other people, which we called the 'zoo'. Amongst the clatter of comptometers and adding machines I was assigned to the pretty important job of tracking and monitoring freight movements between the ACL and other railroads moving through several key junctions. I was doing quite well with a salary of $300 per month, certainly more than I had earned previously. Although it was not the most ideal place to work, I had acquired some clerical skills. The department I worked in was made up of 10 people and was headed up by a very pleasant supervisor who, unlike most supervisors and managers, always wore a suit and necktie.

One day, after I had been with the railroad for about three years, a gentleman came in to call on the manager of the entire section. His appearance was notable because he was dressed in a white linen suit, white shirt, striped necktie and a panama hat. Most impressed, I sought the attention of my supervisor and asked: 'Who is that guy?' He replied that he was the branch manager of the International Business Machines (IBM) office in Raleigh, North Carolina. Having recently read some glowing reports about this company - which was ranked as the most respected and profitable in the world - I immediately made up my mind that I had to go to work for them. I told my supervisor that I wanted an interview with the visitor. He said that was no problem as his brother was the manager of the data processing office and that, through him, he could arrange it. Consequently at 3pm that day, I found myself speaking with Mickey Johnson. His time was limited but he was cordial and suggested that I write him a letter outlining my qualifications and telling him what I thought I could offer IBM.

I wrote the letter but was pessimistic that anything positive would come out of it because it appeared to me that entry into IBM required, at a minimum, a college degree. Lady Luck, however, was smiling on me. One Friday night shortly thereafter, I arrived home from work and was mowing our lawn around the house that we had recently

169

acquired for the sum of $8,200 when Rosalie came to the window and shouted that a man from Raleigh wanted to talk to me on the phone. It was Mickey Johnson. He asked me if I could be in Raleigh the next morning for an interview with his office manager, Marshall Lancaster. As it was only about an hour and a half's drive away, I assured Mr Johnson that I would be in Raleigh at 7am. He said that was not necessary as the meeting with Mr Lancaster was set for 9am to which I replied: 'I'll still be in Raleigh by 7am.'

Oh dear! Rosalie and I began to panic. I did not own a suit, nor a white shirt and not even a decent necktie. What were we to do? The stores were closed but an idea struck us. We knew the owner of a clothing store and I phoned him at his home. He understood the dilemma and told me to meet him in 30 minutes at the store. He outfitted me with a suit, white shirt, striped necktie and a straw hat. No alterations were required so I was set to go. He even told me that I could pay him later and wished me good luck and God speed.

At 9am I was parked in the lot adjacent to the IBM building awaiting the arrival of Mr Lancaster who turned out to be, like me, a New Yorker. A clerk in the office had recently been promoted to a supervisory position in the Atlanta Branch office, which created an opening in Raleigh. After a two-hour interview, he told me that if I could pass the required physical exam, I was hired. The starting salary would be $275 a month but the benefits were outstanding and I jumped at the offer.

Jean and Joan had just started in the first grade and it was the beginning of the new school year. We were beginning a whole new segment of our lives.

The years rolled by. My career with IBM necessitated a number of moves. We moved to Raleigh, North Carolina, then to Greensboro, North Carolina where we anchored for five years. The girls were doing well in school and I had become very active supporting Monsignor Dolan in our Roman Catholic Church. Under his leadership and direction, I do believe that I may have become the first Lector (reader of assigned parts of the liturgy) in the Catholic Church in the United States. I also became involved in 'Toastmasters', where I picked up the much-needed skill of public speaking, which was to become an important part of my IBM career.

We moved on to Richmond, Virginia where we found a really nice house in the suburb of Bon Air but our time there was short-lived owing to my rapidly moving career.

I thought the next move to northern New Jersey might have been difficult for my southern family, but to the contrary, Jean and Joan found Bayley Ellard High School to their liking and Sharon found similar joy in the posh St Elizabeth's Academy in nearby Convent Station –

established in 1860 and the oldest secondary school for young women in New Jersey. Once again we found a delightful house in Morristown, a small town in Morris County.

At the same time that I transferred to IBM's Corporation Headquarters in Armonk, New York, Jean and Joan enrolled in Nursing School at the Holy Name Medical Center in Teaneck, New Jersey. Once more we packed up and this time moved to Stamford, Connecticut.

Sharon in the meantime went off to the University of South Carolina in Columbia where for the first time became fiscally responsible. Up until that time, I think she thought those Weeping Willows I planted in our back yard were money trees. A wonderful experience occurred when we drove her down to Columbia. I searched for someone to take funds for tuition and housing but everyone brushed me off. The next week, Sharon phoned me to tell me that the University wanted payment for those items. It seemed that the University took the position that the student was the customer and therefore responsible for payment. Sharon opened a bank account to which I contributed and we maintained it at an agreed balance. Being obliged to pay her own bills, she instantly became fiscally responsible and embraced the virtue of thrift.

Our spacious home on Mill Road in Stamford was very comfortable. It included a large recreation room on the lower level, which opened to the back yard. When wedding bells became apparent we reasoned that we had sufficient space to hold the receptions at home. Joan was the first, followed shortly thereafter by Jean, and a few years later, Sharon completed the cycle. Having some familiarity with business enterprises in near-by White Plains, New York, our friend Ed Lyons, proprietor of Lyons Bar and Grill volunteered to provide beverages at cost and even loaned us his talented cook.

Our duty as parents took on a different tone. Having been a full-time - and excellent and caring - mom for many years Rosalie was now at home alone for most of her days. Her passion for reading (she read a book a day) led her to take a job in the book department of the upscale Bloomingdale Department Store in Stamford. This literary outlet served a diverse clientele, which included Paul Newman, Joanne Woodward and Alan Alda.

After the girls left, Rosalie and I drifted apart and, after 28 years of marriage during which she had supported me fully in my career and in the bringing up of our three children, the empty nest syndrome contributed to an amicable divorce. She decided to return to her original home in Wilmington, North Carolina.

My career with IBM was rewarding, starting out as a Clerk in a Branch Office, 27 years later, according to the Director I reported to, I was ranked in the top 5% of the company. For several years, my office was located in North Tarrytown, NY but I spent much of my time travelling throughout Asia. My favorite destination was Singapore so I decided that I would move there and establish a business, which I did 8 days after I retired.

My personal life took a dramatic about- turn just three months after moving to Singapore. On May 1, (Labor Day) I went to the Singapore Botanic Gardens and sat under a big tree to finish a book I was reading. It began to rain but I reasoned that I was protected under the shelter of the tree until the rain stopped. Well the rain did not stop and when the tree became saturated I took off and ran to the teahouse on the property, which was full of people who had earlier taken refuge from the downpour. A waiter who was trying to be helpful approached a woman and her two beautiful young daughters and asked if I could sit at their table. She consented and that began a wonderful new experience. Sally had lost her husband to cancer a year earlier and she was left to care for her family, Selvi (14) and Meena (9). The rain continued long enough to establish a friendship. We discovered we shared a love of music, food, travel, tennis and many other things, which led to courtship, and, a few years later, marriage.

My new family quickly became a delight and I came to love Selvi and Meena as much as my own children back in the US. They did not require much discipline and getting them through school was not too difficult. They both married and presented us with two grandchildren each. We love to spend time with them, and though as spoiled as any other kids of their age, they understand that 'Grandpa' is the boss and it is a joy to take long walks with them, preferably one or two at a time.

The Singapore Symphony Orchestra attracts talent from all over the world. I am cultivating the grandkids to appreciate this as much as I do, but have discovered that it is best to take one at a time.

CHAPTER TWELVE

RETURN TO TIANJIN

During the years that had passed since I had been a Marine in China this country remained close to my heart and I harbored a deep desire to return. I watched with sadness all the upheavals - including the Cultural Revolution of the 1970s - that tore its citizens apart and longed for the day when China would again rise and take its place on the world stage. As this came about - slowly at first and then with breath-taking and exponential speed - my yearning to return to China grew apace.

Sally and I visited China - with a fleeting visit to Tianjin - in 2008 (as discussed in the introduction to this memoir) and had every intention to return. However, we got caught up in the routine of our life and did not put specific plans in place.

Except for the three months we spent in Singapore and Australia, the rest of the year 2009 was spent in Vermont. Since Sally had never been to Boston and had no conception of what a 'Cape' was (as in Cape Cod), I took her on an eight-day trip to those areas in the balmy month of September. We had a grand time and mentioned that to Joan Stanbury via email, whereupon she asked for a detailed report of our travels, which I dutifully wrote and sent to her. Her reply showed a deep appreciation of my descriptions of the glories of New England and she expressed a wish to see it all some day.

That set in motion another great experience. Joan has treated us to so many wonderful adventures in Australia that we wanted to do something special for her. We mapped out an 18-day tour all around New England in June 2010 and sent it to her along with an invitation to join us. She was at the travel agent's office the following day, booking her flight tickets.

We started our journey by traveling to Alexandria in the northwestern part of New York State where the Saint Lawrence River comes down from Canada and enters into Lake Ontario in the US. We boarded the beautiful Alexandria Belle out of Uncle Sam's Boat Tours for the journey through 1,865 of the most beautiful islands one could imagine. Each one had one main house - more like castles than houses - and some smaller buildings to accommodate guests as well as a variety of ancillary buildings like gardeners cottages, boathouses, gazebos and fanciful children's play rooms. Our skipper maneuvered skillfully in between US and Canadian waters while we were given a running commentary on the history and highlights of the river. It was the first week of June and we had scored wonderful weather. The day ended with dinner at a homely but excellent German restaurant where fellow guests chatted and made us feel very much part of the local scene.

From Alexandria, we skipped along south of the New York State/Canadian border across to the Lake Champlain area and down to the amazing Shelburne Museum, just south of Burlington, Vermont. I often refer to Joan as a Museum freak as she studies them all over the world, thoroughly enjoying her visits. At Shelburne, she revealed her knowledge - and veneration - of Electra Havemeyer-Webb, the indefatigable founder of the museum and regaled the guides on the history of many of the things that were on display. I think some of them learned a few things from Joan. (Before joining us, she had done her homework.) The sight of the 220 ft. long Ticonderoga, America's last remaining side-paddle-wheel passenger steamer, up on the chocks at the museum fascinated her. She spoke at length with the guides on board who explained how, in 1955, it was hauled on a railway carriage resting on specially-laid tracks two miles overland from Lake Champlain to the museum. Its path took it across highways, over a swamp, through woods and fields and across the tracks of the Rutland Railway. A truly staggering accomplishment and one of the world's greatest feats of maritime preservation.

From Shelburne, we drove north to the Trapp Family Lodge, in Stowe, Vermont and re-lived the dramatic and romantic back-story of 'The Sound of Music' through the relics and photographs displayed in the down-stairs museum.

The next day, we traversed the northern part of Vermont and hooked up with the scenic Kancamangus Trail, which brought us to North Conway deep in the heart of the White Mountains of New Hampshire. We did not go up to the peak of Mount Washington as if was fogged in, but had a fabulous dinner in the 1785 Inn and Restaurant (named for the year it opened). Surely it is one of America's oldest restaurants and its history is reflected in the menu, which seamlessly blends traditional fare with the most modern culinary offerings.

Bar Harbor, Maine on Mount Desert Island was our next port of call. We spent two days there and could have stayed a week because there is so much to see and do. We drove round the island and then took a trolley tour so that we could learn more from the commentary, sprinkled with humour, delivered by the driver. This gave us the opportunity to drench ourselves in history once again while enjoying the delights of Acadia National Park. Having hit the seafood-rich coast, we wasted no time in sampling

Maine lobster and I doubt there was a meal during our visit at which it did not take a starring role.

We then headed south along the rugged Maine coast. Our next overnight was in Camden where, in 1947, 20th Century Fox filmed Grace Metalious's scandalous novel, Peyton Place. We stayed at the 40-room, historic Whitehall Inn, which was built in 1834 as a sea captain's house. Due to the ambiance and delightful owners – it is more like a private home than a hotel - this was our favorite overnight stay of the trip.

The following day we did some whale watching out of Booth Bay Harbor, before leaving for Portland where we had a cross-harbor view of the Navy Marine Corps prison - a magnificent castle-like building which was occupied from 1908 until 1974. Although a number of uses for the building have been suggested since, probably because of lead-paint and asbestos problems, none has come to fruition. That night we had another award winning dinner - on Di Millo's famous floating restaurant.

The next stop was Portsmouth on the Piscataqua River, New Hampshire where Sally spotted the Rusty Hammer restaurant, which we found to be great. While there, we went on board an old submarine, Albacore which served the US Navy from 1953 to 1972. The claustrophobic interior of the vessel made me glad that I did not have to be rescued by one way back in my Marine Corps days.

On to Boston. Having driven in Boston in years gone by and knowing the difficulties it can present, we elected to stay at Braintree, which is to the south and connected to the city by fast train, for the two nights we were there. We did the Freedom Walk and hop-on-hop-off bus tours all around this historical city, stopping by one of our favorite restaurants in the North Side (Little Italy), the Bella Vista. The maitre'D, a delightful man of Italian heritage, never allowed a smile to crack his countenance but kept everyone around him bubbling with mirth with his wry, witty repartee.

After two packed days in Boston we were ready to take on Cape Cod. We drove to Hyannis and checked into the Heritage House, which is within walking distance of the ferries. Since we wanted to go to both Nantucket and Martha's Vineyard, where hotel rooms were available starting around $400/night, we elected to stay in Hyannis and took the early morning ferry to Nantucket one day and the evening ferry back to Hyannis. The Lonely Planet Guide Book says: 'You don't have to be a millionaire to visit Nantucket, but it helps'.

With Australian friends who are descendants of a Nantucket whale hunter by the name of Whippy who jumped ship and settled in Fiji, Joan was on a mission to search out some

181

background information for the family. She found the Nantucket Historical Society most helpful and enjoyed her visit there - coming away with armfuls of photocopies.

On the second day we once again took the early ferry, but this time to Martha's Vineyard. On this charming island, which Sally and I have visited before, we took the local buses which go everywhere at a full day's cost of $3.50. Our favorite spot on the Vineyard is the fishing village of Menensha. There are a handful of seafood shacks right on the water, which serve the greatest lunches ever. The lobster bisque is fresh from the sea and made by the fishermen who catch the crustaceans and the bread rolls are still hot from the village bakery. Another treat on the way back to our hotel was picking up lobster salads at Spanky's Seafood Shack to be enjoyed before being returned to reality with the evening news on TV. What point is there being in this lobster rich area without making the most of it?

Following two great days in Hyannis and the islands, we struck out for Newport, Rhode Island. Our first visit was to the International Tennis Hall of Fame, followed by multiple drives along Belmont Avenue, historic Ocean Drive and past St Mary's church where JFK and Jacqueline Lee Bouvier were married in 1953. We were terribly disappointed that that one of my favorite restaurants in Newport served up some smelly mussels that we had to send back. That dampened our spirits for the night, however we chose other items from the menu and were satisfied.

Sally chose to spend a bit of time in the casino while Joan and I did the famous Cliff Walk, with the majestic Atlantic Ocean on one side and a plethora of elegant, but apparently unoccupied, mansions on the other side. A visit to the harbor-side New York Yacht Club's headquarters in Newport, the former home of the Brown family of Brown University fame, co-incided with the registration day for the Newport to Bermuda yacht race. We enjoyed talking with some of the skippers though we did not have the opportunity of seeing their sail boats.

Our final stop on the home run was the Norman Rockwell Museum in Stockbridge, Massachusetts. We gazed in awe at original copies of his pithy, often comical and always topical 321 cover paintings for the Saturday Evening Post. Sally and I had the pleasure of introducing Joan to Rockwell's Four Freedom series painted in 1943 during World War II. Inspired by a speech by Franklin D. Roosevelt, they were pictorial representations of the four principles of universal rights - freedom from want, freedom of speech, freedom of worship and freedom from fear. Oh that all the leaders of the world would take heed of these human rights.

Joan, being an avid and experienced traveller, recorded

every detail of our New England excursion and wrote an 18-page diary of our trip. I re-read it often to remind myself of what a great visit we had. As the driving force behind this memoir, Joan also sat down at my computer and framed the titles of nine chapters covering my earlier days in China and gently suggested (with a hint of steel in her voice) that I fill in the blanks. The chapters are not exactly the way she lined them up but the fire was lit and I agreed to proceed with what turned out to be a labor of love. With all the China Marines - and other members of that illustrious company – this exercise has certainly enriched the latter part of my life.

Reinvigorated, Sally and I took off for Singapore and China for the months of September and October of 2010. We allocated one more day to explore Tianjin in quest of the vestiges I sought. This time, we tried the phone number given to us at the end of our previous visit and although the dialect was a bit confusing, got a street address and hailed a taxi. Upon reaching our destination, we did not find the address given but fate was on our side. As I wandered around, in the next street I saw a building which looked familiar and upon closer inspection discovered that indeed it was the office building we had occupied in 1945. It was now a government office building so we were not allowed to go in but I was elated that we had made the discovery.

We then set out, using taxis, trying to find the house I lived in and once again, we struck out. By mid-afternoon we were discouraged again, so I consulted my Lonely Planet guidebook for hints. This resulted in locating The Board of Tourism office. They advised us that they were not in the business of providing tour guides but once more we were touched by the friendliness that the Chinese extended to us. The receptionist said she knew a man who might be willing to take us around the city and phoned him. He is a fine gentleman with a big car and the price was right so went about our search for the elusive house.

Our new friend had had a lot of experience helping Americans and Europeans who lived in Tianjin before the Mao years and thought he could be of help. He and I were obsessed with finding the house so we explored one street after another but could not find any building even resembling our temporary home. We did locate the main barracks where most of our troops were billeted. This provided more confidence so we decided to go back to the site of the old office and wander from there to see what we could find. We rounded a corner and I saw something that struck a chord. I asked if that was still a hotel. Our escort confirmed that it was the Astor Hotel and we could access it by driving around the corner to the entrance of a multi-story addition that had been attached on the river side of the original building. We entered the hotel and asked if we could wander around the old section. They graciously provided a very polite lady to show us around. As soon as I entered what was the old lobby, I knew where we were and the location of the room I occupied 66 years ago. I remembered that because it was the last room down the hall and was opposite the elevator – now out of use, but preserved in its original condition. Sure enough it was there. We spotted a sign that said 'Museum' and asked if we could visit it. There we found a lovely young woman by the name of Sherry Gao. She showed us around, and we took many photos, including one of Major General Keller E Rockey signing the surrender document, which liberated North China from Japanese occupation. We were on a roll but realized that we were up against a time limit as we had reservations on a train back to Beijing and had to cut our visit short. We vowed to resume our research another day.

Fast forward to October 2011. Joan flew up to Singapore and spent a few days there with us before we three ventured into China with the express intent of wrapping up the re-discovery of where I had been 66 years previously. We flew into Beijing late on Sunday evening and made our way to the Beijing hotel - chosen because it was close to the US Embassy, which we intended to visit later in the week. The hotel has a restaurant, operated by a gentleman from the Middle East, who offered a comprehensive menu along with deliciously strong Arabic coffee. Joan was amused by the fact that she, an Australian, was eating a Spanish omelet prepared by a Lebanese in Beijing with me, an American and Sally a Chinese while chatting with a well-educated, multi-lingual Mongolian gentleman sitting at the next table. An international breakfast, indeed.

The next day was spent settling in, doing a bit of shopping and enjoying the hospitality and beauty of the city. Sally and I had been in Beijing in 2008 and again in 2010. Joan had also been there before. On previous visits, we were confronted with pollution that enveloped the city, the sun red and so heavily veiled that it could be viewed by the naked eye. This time, however, we were in for a wonderful surprise. The air quality was magnificent, with clear skies and a dazzling sun.

China has done an amazing job of importing trees, which make their own food from carbon dioxide in the atmosphere. In the process, they release oxygen for us to breathe. They help to settle out, trap and hold particle pollutants such as dust, ash, pollen, and smoke that can damage human lungs. Trees produce enough oxygen on each acre for about 18 people every day. As we traveled around the cities, we saw tree farms on virtually every piece of vacant land. They start with young plants and when more mature, transplant them to the permanent locations. This contributes to a cleaner, healthier atmosphere, while adding to the beauty of the municipalities. In addition to the

187

trees, masses of flowers adorned overpasses, nature-strips alongside roadways, sidewalks, parks, and gardens. They were virtually everywhere and fed my increasing love affair with a country I had known under very different circumstances many years before.

Early Tuesday morning, we headed out to Tianjin, where I had much research to do for this book. We caught a taxi to take us to the Beijing South Railway Station. Even though it was early morning, we found the ride totally without stress as we passed along freeways lined by flowering rose bushes and other plants in bloom.

We had been to the Beijing South Station the previous year but were still impressed by its immense size and splendor. Finding our way to purchase tickets was not difficult as the directional signs were very explicit and for the most part, in English as well as Chinese. Sally's knowledge of the language significantly eased the pathway. Locating the correct gate at first was a bit tricky but soon it all made sense and we arrived with plenty of time to spare. What a contrast this was to the time Sally and I risked life and limb through an antique station, which was severely lacking in every possible way (only three years prior). This time everyone proceeded in an orderly manner and we were comfortably seated on the high-speed train. At the stroke of 11:30 we eased out of the station and soon were experiencing the speed of 294 kilometers an hour. The 30-

minute journey took us through the southern part of Beijing, then through some industrial complexes. Followed by neat farms and occasional housing estates, pristine rivers and canals, through dozens of tree farms, then the outskirts and finally slid into another beautiful station of Tianjin. I spared a thought for my China Marine friend John Ahigian of Boston and Cape Cod who had taken more than 12 hours to cover the same distance, in frightening circumstances, in 1945.

We somehow managed to miss the normal taxi loading area but did find plenty of willing taxi drivers to take us to the hotel. I was a bit suspect that they were not in the normal taxi queue and soon learned the reason why. These chaps were not inclined to use their meters and were intent on charging a higher fare. Since I knew how close we were to the hotel, I was not going to be bullied into an exorbitant rate for the short ride, but we managed to bargain one driver down to a reasonable fare.

Our travel agent had booked us into the Astor Plaza, a sister hotel to the Astor Hotel. The Astor Hotel is a five star hotel (under-rated in my opinion) and the Plaza is a four star hotel (also under-rated) and considerably cheaper. Its rooms were very comfortable and the only thing missing was a connection to Wi-Fi, which I needed for my iPad. The receptionist showed us a corridor that linked the two hotels -

all I needed to do was to go over to the public area of the Astor Hotel and I was in business.

Naturally, the first thing we did after checking in was to rush over to the Museum in the basement of the Astor Hotel to visit our friend Sherry Gao. She was more than delighted to see us since, after our departure the previous year, she had notified the founder of the Museum, Mr He Huan Zhen and other dignitaries of our visit and they had expressed great interest, saying if we made a second visit they would like to meet us. It was becoming clear that not only Americans were unaware of our Untold War Story, the Chinese were also eager to learn more about this period of history.

Sherry contacted Mr He as well as Mr Kevin Zhao, who was affiliated with the Board of Tourism, and the Hotel General Manager, Mr Leon Jen Lee who came to meet me and to hear my personal story. They expressed great interest in my project and are looking forward to the release of this book.

At the invitation of the Board of Tourism, Sally and I moved from our room in the Plaza to the room I occupied in 1945. What a wonderful experience. As an example of the quality of that magnificent hotel, the parquet floor and the armoire dresser were the same as when I last occupied that room.

190

The Astor Hotel has a fascinating history and it is commendable that the civic authorities in Tianjin have chosen to preserve it.

In 1860, The British and French negotiated a treaty with the Qing government, which opened the Tientsin Port to foreign trade. Following the signing of the treaty, a considerable amount of land was provided for permanent lease, which was to become the British, French and American Concessions. In the British Concession the Deputy Consul for Tientsin, John Gibson established a municipal council, known as The Board, to govern the concession.

John Innocent, a British missionary and member of the United Methodist Mission, arrived in Tientsin in May 1861 and quickly became involved with the work of the The Board.

Property and land were transferred from The Board to private businesses by way of Crown Lease. In 1863, Innocent signed a Crown Lease agreement with Deputy Consul Gibson, and purchased a plot of land in the British concession. The money was raised from Innocent's missionary income.

After acquiring the lease, Innocent began to develop the land, first by building some single-story houses; which were used as storehouses, offices and a hotel. The hotel was to become the first international hotel in modern Chinese history, The Astor Hotel.

Between the opening of the original hotel in 1863, and the end of the century, the Astor became an important venue for diplomatic activity. The British Consulate regularly held meetings there and the American Consulate was established in the hotel, and remained there until 1929.

Following the establishment of the hotel, Innocent concentrated much of his energy on the development of Christianity in Tientsin, using some of the hotel profits to provide financial support for his missionary work and thus repaying some of the original investment from missionary funds.

In 1886, renovation and extension work began on The Astor Hotel. From a one-story building it grew to a three-level structure with a veranda and tower overlooking Victoria Park. The classical west-European styling distinguished the hotel as the most impressive building in Tientsin until the beginning of the 20th century. The setting was ideal, situated between Victoria Park to the west and the Haihe River on the east.

The original concessions of Tientsin have had a direct influence upon the development of modern Tianjin society. Reconstruction of the hotel became a major milestone in the architectural history of the city. The hotel architecture was the benchmark, emulated by many companies including banks. Buildings constructed during this period reflected both western and Chinese styles. This gave Tientsin a world-renowned reputation for distinctive building styles which influenced international architecture.

During the Boxer Revolution, the hotel came under fire repeatedly and considerable damage was done. For a time, the hotel was shut down while repairs were made and by the time the rebellion had been put down, things were back to normal. With its elegant design and the salubrious surroundings the Astor was again attracting a multitude of famous guests from both China and abroad.

By 1900, the hotel continued to demonstrate its forward outlook. It led the way in the introduction of modern facilities to China. It was many years after the Astor Hotel was equipped with electricity that other buildings began to follow. It also was the first hotel to install a heating system, in 1905 and a hot water boiler, in 1910. The boiler was the most advanced in the world and could supply the guests with hot water round the clock.

For decades that followed, the Astor Hotel served some of the most powerful and influential persons from all over the world; perhaps the most notable was Dr Sun Yat-sen.

During the Japanese occupation of China, they controlled much of China and in 1943 actually took over the Astor

Hotel, with General Uchida, Commander of the Japanese Occupation Army named as Manager. He re-named it The Asian Hotel.

The surrender of North China to the United States Marine Corps in 1945, on behalf of Generalissimo Kai-shek, removed any claim by the Japanese to the hotel. After the surrender, the Chinese National Party resumed control over 934 Japanese occupied facilities and 94 facilities on behalf of Britain and the United States, including the Astor Hotel. William O'Hara, a British subject had been The Astor Hotel's General Manager until he and his wife were taken to a concentration camp in Wei County. After his release, they returned and he resumed his role as General Manager and majority shareholder.

Following the Second World War, a full-scale civil war broke out in China. By the end of November, 1948 the People's Liberation Army advanced toward Tientsin and by January 1949 Tientsin was liberated.

With the founding of the People's Republic of China in 1949, The Astor Hotel was again faced with a period of uncertainty. The warlords, businessmen and high officials of the previous years were rapidly departing. With the bombardment of the hotel during the liberation battle and the tearing down of the British flag from the mast of the Astor, there was a deep sense of despair and foreboding within the hotel community. Most of the westerners who had been long-term residents of Tientsin were packing to return to their homes.

The hotel, which had been prosperous for nearly one hundred years, became deserted. In 1951 less than forty percent of the rooms were occupied and in 1952 the hotel received only two guests throughout the entire year. Guests were absent, financial resources were exhausted and the hotel became in arrears with tax payments to the government. Becoming desperate, O'Hara could find no way to re-establish the former prosperity of the hotel. The board held a meeting and it was decided that in view of the state of business and the situation in Tientsin, all of the hotel's assets, including creditors rights and debts would be handed over to the People's Government. Sadly William O'Hara, who had been associated with the hotel for fifty years, was now penniless. He and his wife left China and traveled to New Zealand in search of a new life. He died a year later, never returning to England.

With the development of a new socialist society in China many problems had to be resolved. The Astor Hotel after an initial period of uncertainty, gradually found the correct way to progress with its development. Over the 30-year period from the take-over of the hotel it continued to develop and play an active role in Tientsin life. The hotel received many different foreign delegations and heads of state, as well as senior members of the Chinese Central Committee.

The 'Great Cultural Revolution' was a decade of turmoil, ignorance and a devaluing of civilization. However the errors of this period were soon realized and methods to correct the situation were taken. The end of the Cultural Revolution brought a thirst for learning and knowledge, culture, science and technology.

Once again the hotel had survived an initial period of change and emerged strong and prosperous, earning much praise and respect.

With the opening of China to the outside world, the management of the hotel quickly understood the benefits of co-operation with a foreign partner, which would bring additional expertise and investment. Therefore, in March 1984 the hotel became the first in Tianjin to establish a joint venture when the General Tourist Company of Tianjin signed an agreement with the Zapata Trading Company of Hong Kong. The agreement called for re-construction of the hotel in the original classical British style, with modern facilities and management.

Renovation of the two old buildings and a new wing was begun in 1985. The new seven-story, luxury wing was completed in 1987 and opened by the leaders of the Tianjin Municipal Government. The Astor Hotel is famous for its wide selection of both western and Chinese restaurants, each with its own style and charm.

The Astor Plaza is a 14-story building adjacent to the Astor Hotel, which was built in 1999. It is a bit more modest than the Astor but is a fine addition to the Astor Hotel family.

Having taken in the splendor of this magnificent hotel and all of the fine people associated with it, we were ready to retrace our steps back to Beijing. We made our way to the train station and boarded the high-speed train for the journey through the scenic countryside.

We arrived back in Beijing and that night had a delicious Chinese banquet at a restaurant owned by a very special friend, Brad Huang. Brad is a Chinese American citizen who had migrated back to his home city to take advantage of the booming prosperity of modern China. We were treated to a wonderful assortment of Chinese dishes - some we had never seen or tasted before. Brad had also invited Chuck Yu to join us, which made for a great visit with two of our favorite people in China.

The next day, we visited the United States Embassy to report on what we had been doing in Tianjin. The embassy building, of fairly recent construction, is amongst a group of foreign embassies in the north-east of Beijing and is heavily fortified. Initially one must walk up a road - closed to vehicular traffic - and through a gate similar to an airport checkpoint. Passports and reasons for the visit are checked and handbags, brief cases and other hand luggage is passed through X-ray machines with cameras, batteries, mobile phones, iPads and any other banned items put into secure lockers to be collected when leaving. Visitors then cross a paved and elegantly landscaped courtyard to another entrance. Here visitors again show passports, give reasons for the visit and nominate the person with whom they have an appointment before going through another checkpoint. 'Visitor' labels, printed with personal information, are attached to their lapels. Under the watchful eye of Marines on duty and other security personnel they are offered a seat, coffee and magazines to read while awaiting their appointment time. Before too long they are joined by the person who is expecting them and led through yet another check-point into the embassy proper.

We had been invited to the embassy for me to deliver a talk about my China Marine experience immediately after World War II to a meeting of about a dozen folk. They included embassy officials and a couple of young Marines on duty in China whose eyes were on stalks as I told of my experiences there so many moons ago. It certainly was a different world and one of which they had little knowledge. They were all fascinated by my stories and asked many questions. Over the hour or so we spent at the meeting, I felt a little like a walking history book and searched every corner of my memory to respond to their queries as accurately - and colorfully - as I possibly could.

Our visit coincided with a special day at the embassy - an annual event to which the Ambassador invited quality vendors from all over Beijing to present their wares at a market place set up in the grand hall of the Embassy. With magnificent portraits of famous figures in American history looking down it was a scene of much activity - with the market stall owners responding to the dignity of their surroundings and offering their goods with restraint and good humor to appreciative embassy staff. We were invited to share in the commercial activity and both Joan and Sally chose to buy some exquisite jade jewelry. It was an unexpected bonus to our embassy visit.

When Sally and I had visited the embassy the previous year, Ambassador Jon Huntsman Jr was attending to affairs elsewhere so we did not have the opportunity to meet with him. We first met Jon when he was Ambassador to the Republic of Singapore, several years before and renewed acquaintances with him and his charming family in Park City, Utah, and actually worked on his successful campaign for the governorship of the State of Utah. When we were in Singapore and again in Park City, he was always interested in chatting with Sally in Mandarin, which he handles well.

Colonel Mike McCallus, Defense Liaison Officer, presented

a medallion to me, which is representative of the Defense Attaché's office in Beijing. He also showed us the American Flag which was in the office of the Military Attaché of the US Embassy in Beijing when the Japanese came in on December 8, 1941- the day after they had bombed Pearl Harbor. The Japanese entered the compound and ordered that the flag be struck (taken down) at 1pm. The Assistant Military Attaché refused to strike the flag until the normal time, which was 5pm. At that time, the flag was lowered and presented to him. He returned it to the US Embassy in Beijing in 1964 and it is framed and mounted in the current embassy.

Our research mission in China was now at an end so we flew out the next day, Sally and me to Singapore with plans to spend a little time with the family before returning to US. Joan continued on to her home in Noosa Heads, Australia.

We look forward to our next trip to China to present copies of this book to add to the rich collection of history and historical memorabilia at both the embassy and the museum at The Astor Hotel, thereby sharing this bit of untold history with the fine people of China and those who serve our country at the American Embassy there.

At this stage Sally and I were still living in Vermont. I had been yearning to move back to Singapore for some years but Sally was reluctant to give up her relationships with the wonderful people who came to her for alterations. As her expertise and excellent reputation in the town of Manchester and surrounding districts had become known (word-of-mouth is the best advertisement) she had expanded from not only doing alterations for the up-market men's and women's clothes outlets but, on occasions, was asked to mend such odd things as dog jackets and horse blankets. There was a constant stream of men at the door asking her to raise of lower the hems or take in or let out their jeans. Some, both men and women, even came with a hopeless look in their eyes and asked her to sew on a button. She loved whatever task was given her and never went to bed at night until all the work that had come in that day had been attended to.

As well Sally had established contact with a team of tennis players and they played furiously competitive games, sometimes seven mornings in the week, in Manchester. She could not believe that her life could be better – working for about nine months of the year and spending the rest in Singapore with her daughters and grandchildren or traveling elsewhere in the world.

It took much persuasion on my part, but, eventually Sally consented to head 'home' to Singapore. The US had been our main residence for the past 13 years.

In September 2013 we packed up, shipped our goods to Singapore and flew home. It was wonderful to be back with the family - they are particularly fond of our walks in this wonderful 'walking city' and going with us to The American Club, where I maintain membership. The Olympic-sized swimming pool is draw-card for them.

Being an admirer of the symphony, I try not to miss too many opportunities to enjoy performances at the Concert Hall, which has been acclaimed by well-known performers as one of the finest venues in the world, in addition to the extremely talented local musicians.

CHAPTER THIRTEEN

CHINA MARINE ASSOCIATION

In 1989, a group of dedicated Marines got together to form an organization, which included those Marines who had served in China during the period 1898 - 1949. In attempting to bring them together they cast their net far and wide to reach as many China Marines as possible, even placing advertisements in newspapers. Since I was living in Singapore, I missed the messages that were circulating in the United States.

When I came back to live in the US, my friend Jerry Labounty introduced me to the organization which I joined. Since we made it a practice to return to our home in Singapore during the summer months, we missed a couple of the annual reunions but we re-arranged our schedule so we could attend the 24th reunion in Fredericksburg, Virginia, the 25th in Branson, Missouri and the 26th in Savannah, Georgia. It is a pity that I did not know about the organization earlier as it constitutes some of the finest Marines who made a significant contribution to our country and to our ally, China.

Time has taken its toll and our numbers are dwindling. At the time of writing this memoir the 27th and final reunion is to be held in Charleston, South Carolina from September 17 to 21 2014.

At the reunions, much of the time is spent by the guys sitting around shooting the breeze about the old days and catching up on things that are going on currently in our personal lives. The organizers do a fabulous job providing some form of a guided tour of the host city and taking advantage of events, which are popular attractions in that area. The Missouri reunion included a great voyage on the Branson Belle, a huge showboat on Table Rock Lake, which included an entertaining series of on-stage performers. In Savannah we were treated to a very special town excursion with a deep-south comedian providing a delightful commentary. As well we – some 200 of us - were bussed to Parris Island where many had gone through boot-camp, to view a Graduation Ceremony. It was spectacular and brought back so many memories.

At the reunions there are always guest speakers and patriotic presentations and, as the years roll on, more and more family members are accompanying their famed fathers, grandfathers and great uncles - not only to make sure they are cared for, but also to pay tribute to their service. One of the most important sessions is a series of tributes paid to those members who have passed away in the previous year. This is highlighted by a musical presentation of 'Taps' by a local member of the militia. Naturally, a business meeting is held for all members, and also a meeting of those especially dedicated individuals who devote endless hours to keep the organization running throughout the year - the Executive Committee. On the last night of the reunion, we have a banquet, the farewell gathering.

Since the organization did not come together until 1989, membership mostly consists of those who served around the time I first went to China and beyond, therefore I did not meet any of the guys I served with during the war. This was a period which was tenuous at best as our representation, in addition to assisting the Chinese to put things in North China back together, was to repatriate many thousands of Japanese safely back to their homeland, and to keep the Communists and the Russians at bay.

A significant contribution not only to China Marines, but the entire Marine Corps, is the documentation of the rich history of the Marine Corps in China from 1854 through 1949, as researched and documented by William J Parker Jr. Bill has served as an officer in the association for several years and has played a major role in performing many duties, effectively holding the organization together. His contributions cannot be overstated. Fortunately, he gets a lot of assistance from his daughter, Bonnie. He currently serves as Editor/Publisher of the Scuttlebutt, a quarterly publication that contains current news about the organization and also stories written by members detailing their experiences while in China.

EPILOGUE

I opened this book with a description of how we came to know and love Joan Stanbury, the most talented and intellectual person I know - without her persistence and encouragement, this book would not exist. It is fitting to close with a few tales of the fun we have shared over the 40 years of our friendship and reflect on the many times we have been welcome guests in the land of her birth, Australia.

My first encounter with Australia was in the days I traveled there on business for the IBM Corporation – which I have attempted to précis in this book. In my position, sometimes I was an advocate for IBM Australia and sometimes an adversary. Australians are by no means shy and often resented (as many subsidiary companies do) the perception of intrusion by the parent corporation. The executives and I had a few skirmishes but for the most part the relationship was wholesome.

After I retired from IBM I continued to travel to Australia on business for Philip Crosby Associates – Far East.

On flights from the United States, Pan Am was my favored carrier. With a Frequent Flyer number 350, the really long flights from Honolulu were pretty comfortable. On flights from Singapore my preferred carrier was Singapore Airlines, on which I also had special privileges. My first port of call was always Sydney and I always arrived at dawn. Flights into Sydney often come from the west over land with the aircraft circling out over the Pacific Ocean before swinging westward for the landing at Kingsford-Smith airport. I have rarely seen more spectacular landings as those I so frequently enjoyed - viewing the magnificent headlands basking in the sparkling, rising sun.

In pre-hijacking days, a few of the airlines allowed one passenger to sit in the cockpit for limited periods during a flight. I often had that privilege and a couple of times I persuaded the pilot to allow me to remain for the landings, which was the icing on the cake. What an experience to witness professionals handle a massive machine with apparent ease! The view from the cockpit as we came in was indeed a special treat. There was one occasion made memorable because of humor. Naturally, the flight deck is in constant contact with the control tower. On this trip, as the pilot made the final turn, the tower asked him if he had a clear view of the landing site. The pilot responded with: 'Yes we have your island in sight'. While it is true that Australia is an island, that particular description appeared to the controller as a 'put-down'. Shortly thereafter, he declared that there was some heavy traffic arriving and, to 'get even', ordered the Pan Am 747 to go around again - and again. The pilot eventually apologized for his joke and we landed safely. You don't mess with them Aussies.

In the 70s, 80s and 90s, my travel to Australia was business-oriented but in recent years, the magnet for Sally and me has been visiting our many friends and participating in one of the finest patriotic events in the entire world – Anzac Day. The word 'Anzac' - an acronym for Australia and New Zealand Army Corps - arose from the combination of the two forces at Gallipoli, Turkey, in World War 1. Since then it has become a sort-of generic word to cover all servicemen and servicewomen in all wars that Australians and New Zealanders have participated. In every city and most country towns throughout Australia and New Zealand, on April 25, a dawn service and a daytime parade is held and in some special spots there is a sunset service as well. Serving personnel, members of the reserve forces, veteran organizations, as well as civic establishments from all over the world come to Sydney to participate in these events.

In 2012, I joined fellow Marines in this patriotic event for the third time and again in 2014 for the fourth time. My truly good friend, Bruce Olsen, a highly decorated Marine of the Vietnam conflict who was introduced to me by Joan, looks after me. He and half a dozen other American Marine Corps veterans had relocated to Australia, where - unlike the unhappy reception they received in the US when they

209

first returned home from Vietnam - they were welcomed and became citizens of that great country.

Amongst the many courtesies extended to veterans who wear their medals or uniforms, all public transport - train, bus or ferry - is complimentary on Anzac Day. We are fortunate that friends of Joan's, Jill and Adrian Lutton, have an apartment in Gordon, a northern suburb of Sydney - we affectionately call it 'The Gordon Hilton' - and vacate their home for us to take up residence for about a week for the Anzac Day march and associated celebrations. Sometimes they move up to their holiday home at Tea Gardens, about three hours north of Sydney; other times they organize an overseas trip at the same time that we will be in Sydney. Without their generosity over the years I would not have been able to participate in so many Anzac Day celebrations. Thank you, Adrian and Jill.

A couple who have an apartment in the same building, Coral and Tom Coughlan, always set up a table in the hallway which pays tribute to Anzac Day and to the US Marines – with photographs and flags. Coral makes us welcome with gifts of cookies or cakes and on one memorable occasion delivered a cake topped with an American flag- in glossy icing. She had put many hours of work into that masterpiece and it was truly appreciated.

On Anzac Day we don't attend the dawn service because

Joan is sensitive to my age and avoids pushing me too much. We catch an early train into Sydney however, so we have plenty of time to locate the staging area assigned to us for the parade – advised in advance by Bruce. While waiting for our turn to march we mingle with other units – there is much warm camaraderie. When called to join the parade we fall in behind the American Legion members and a team of young volunteers who graciously carry our colors. For the next hour or so, with thousands of patriots cheering us on, we follow the leaders through the main streets of Sydney to the beat of bands which intersperse the marching men and women. What a thrill it is to receive such honors from so many people who appreciate the contributions of their - and Allied - veterans.

Toward the end of the parade, Sally and Joan, along with family members and close friends who accompany us but do not march, go ahead and scout out our favorite pub. When we arrive at the finishing point - Hyde Park in central Sydney - we regroup and repair to the chosen pub to cool down, have a drink and socialize with other participants and observers. In a city of five million people it is estimated that about a million people of all ages cheered us on. Oh that such patriotism existed in America!

In 2012, a friend of Joan's, Geoff Luck (she knows everyone) organized for us to be guests of honor at a sunset service at The Beach Club, which is a Returned

Servicemen's Club at Collaroy Beach, a suburb about eight miles north of the city of Sydney. In a salute to my service as a Marine, I was invited to join the formation of veterans on the beach for the ceremony. Some of the Australian veterans, known affectionately as 'Diggers', wore the time-honored slouch hat while others wore the uniforms and/or headgear of their particular service organization.

The ceremony featured a speech by a Federal Member of Parliament followed by a very moving service. A member of the clergy and a military escort carried a wreath down to the water's edge and placed it in a traditional, clinker-built wooden surfboat. The crew - a team of local lifesavers - rowed out beyond the breakers, placed the wreath on the water, stood at attention with their oars aloft and remained there until the sun dipped below the horizon. We veterans, most of whom had made rather heavy work of marching in the beach sand, remained at attention as a bugler played the Last Post.

My nephew Joe, having tired of hearing about our annual trips to Asia and to Australia for Anzac Day had joined us in Sydney and was an interested spectator in the entire Anzac Day memorial traditions - observing the parade and enjoying the camaraderie with fellow Marines at the hotel after the march. He maintained his equilibrium until the sunset service at Collaroy Beach and then the tears flowed. A little discombobulated by his overwhelming reaction - he is a tough guy - Joe wandered a little way down the beach, mopping his eyes as he went. We all felt equally emotional.

The end of the day saw us back at Jill and Adrian's apartment watching media reports of how this spectacular day was observed throughout Australia and New Zealand - from the first dawn service to the last bugle call. It dominated the news bulletins.

As this book is in the final stages of writing, I am in Australia again with Sally and Joan and will be marching with the Marines on Anzac Day, 2014. I don't know how many more years the good Lord is going to allow this aging body and mind to function, but God willing, I will return again and again to pay tribute to those Australians and New Zealanders – more than 10,000 - who made the supreme sacrifice at Gallipoli in World War 1, a century ago.

Do I love Australia and its citizens? You be the judge!

ACKNOWLEDGEMENTS

This untold bit of history would not exist if it were not for the perseverance of my dear friend, Joan Stanbury who tenaciously persuaded me to embark on this venture, then kept me going throughout a long but worthwhile venture.

Next in line for recognition are the contributors: J. Michael Miller, Ted Toole, John Ahigian, and Mike di Monda.

Research was accomplished through the tireless efforts of John Lyles, at the Marine Corps Research Center in Quantico, Virginia assisted by Martha Robertson. Additional research was obtained from the National Archives Center at College Park, Maryland where Archives Specialist, Nathanial Patch performed the same type of service, including a copy of the actual 'Act of Surrender'.

Having shared a copy of the manuscript with a few friends, I received valuable advice, which improved the book. They include Carrie Feron, Bill Payne, and Jim Campbell.

In China, I received support from Sherry Gao, He Huan Zhee, Kevin Zhao, and Leon Jen Lee, all of whom encouraged me to continue my pursuit, and to the folks at the U S Embassy in Beijing.

Moral support and encouragement came from so many that it is impossible to name everyone, and at the risk of overlooking many I wish to acknowledge Joe Messina, Tom Anderer, Jeff Anderson, Alan Greczynski, the Jaussaud family, Josh Nielsont, Bruce Olsen, and Kevin O'Toole, and to my cardiologist Melvin Tan whose care and advice keeps me going.

I am grateful to all of my friends in the China Marine Association, especially Bill Parker and Bonnie Parker who provided historical as well as pictorial data. Finally I am indebted to my talented daughter, Meena for helping to get it print ready along with help from Elaine and Sherry at UNIMAX .

Made in the USA
Monee, IL
20 March 2020